Hong Kong Banking Ordinance

International Law & Taxation Publishers

London

Hong Kong Banking Ordinance

ISBN 1-893713-29-6

Copyright © 2001 International Law & Taxation Publishers

International Law & Taxation Publishers
London

http://www.internationallawandtaxationpublishers.com

Contents

BANKING ORDINANCE

(as amended)

Arrangement of Sections

Part I - Preliminary

Part II - Appointments, Functions Of Monetary Authority, Reports By Monetary Authority And Power Of Governor To Give Directions

Part III - Banking Business And Business Of Taking Deposits To Be Carried On By Authorized Institutions Only

Part IV- Authorization

Part V - Revocation Of Authorization

Part XI - Audits And Meetings

Part XII - Disclosure of Information by Authorized Institutions

Part XIII - Ownership and Management of Authorized Institutions.

Part XIV

Part XV - Limitations on Loans by and Interests of Authorized Institutions

Part XVI - Advertisements, Representations and Use of Title "Bank"

Part XVII - Capital Adequacy Ratio of Authorized Institutions

Part XVIII - Liquidity Ratio of Authorized Institutions and Matters Affecting Liquidity Ratio

Part XXII - Transitional, Savings and Repeal

BANKING

To regulate banking business and the business of taking deposits and to make provision for the supervision of authorized institutions so as to provide a measure of protection to depositors and to promote the general stability and effective working of the banking system, and to provide for matters incidental thereto or connected therewith.

PART I - Preliminary

Short title

1.(1) This Ordinance may be cited as the Banking Ordinance.

(2) (*Omitted as spent*)

Interpretation

2.(1) In this Ordinance, unless the context otherwise requires-

"accounts" means any accounts, whether kept in writing or print or by any machine or device;

"advertisement" means any form of advertising, whether notified or published-

> *(a)* in a newspaper, magazine, journal or other periodical publication;
>
> *(b)* by the display of posters or notices;
>
> *(c)* by means of circulars, brochures, pamphlets or handbills;
>
> *(d)* by an exhibition of photographs or cinematograph films; or
>
> *(e)* by way of sound broadcasting or television,

and references to the issue of an advertisement shall be construed accordingly;

"Advisor", in relation to an authorized institution, means the person appointed, pursuant to section 52(1)(B), to be the Advisor of the institution;

"approved currency" means a currency-

> *(a)* freely convertible into Hong Kong dollars; or
>
> *(b)* approved by the Monetary Authority;

"associate", in relation to a person entitled to exercise, or control the exercise of, voting power in relation to, or holding shares in, a company, means any other person in respect of whom that first-mentioned person has an agreement or arrangement, whether oral or in writing, express or implied, with respect to the acquisition, holding or disposal of shares or other interests in that company or under which they act together in exercising their voting power in relation to it;

"auditor" means a professional accountant holding a practising certificate under the Professional Accountants Ordinance (Cap. 50);

"authorization" means, as the case requires-

(a)   the authorization under section 16 of a company to carry on banking business, a business of taking deposits as a deposit-taking company or a business of taking deposits as a restricted licence bank, as the case may be;

(b)   the banking licence, registration or restricted banking licence, as the case may be, held by an authorized institution;

"authorized institution" means-

(a)   a bank;

(b)   a restricted licence bank; or

(c)   a deposit-taking company;

"authorized institution incorporated in Hong Kong" means an authorized institution incorporated in Hong Kong by or under the Companies Ordinance (Cap. 32) or any other Ordinance and any reference to a bank incorporated in Hong Kong, a deposit-taking company incorporated in Hong Kong or a restricted licence bank incorporated in Hong Kong shall be construed accordingly;

"authorized institution incorporated outside Hong Kong" means an authorized institution incorporated by or under the law or other authority in any place outside Hong Kong;

"automated teller machine" means a terminal device, whether installed by a bank or by some other person, which is linked directly or indirectly to a computer system used by a bank and which provides facilities to customers of the bank;
"bank" means a company which holds a valid banking licence;

"Banking Advisory Committee" means the Banking Advisory Committee established by section 4;

"banking business" means the business of either or both of the following-

(a)   receiving from the general public money on current, deposit, savings or other similar account repayable on demand or within less than 3 months or at call or notice of less than 3 months;

(b) paying or collecting cheques drawn by or paid in by customers;

"banking licence" means a banking licence granted under section 16;

"capital adequacy ratio" means the capital adequacy ratio referred to in section 98;

"chief executive", in relation to an authorized institution, means the chief executive appointed under section 74 in respect of the institution, and includes an alternate chief executive so appointed;

"company" means a body corporate-

(a) incorporated under the Companies Ordinance (Cap. 32);

(b) incorporated by any other Ordinance; or

(c) incorporated outside Hong Kong;

"controller", in relation to a company-

(a) means, in respect of all the provisions of this Ordinance, any person who is-

    (i) an indirect controller; or

    (ii) a majority shareholder controller; and

(b) includes, in respect of the provisions of Part XIII, any person who is a minority shareholder controller,

of that company, and references in this Ordinance to "control" shall be construed accordingly;

"currency" includes-

(a) the European Currency Unit; and

(b) any medium of exchange the subject of a declaration under subsection (5)(a) which is in force;

"deposit" -

(a) means a loan of money-

      (i)   at interest, at no interest or at negative interest; or

      (ii)   repayable at a premium or repayable with any consideration in money or money's worth; but

   (b)   does not include a loan of money-

      (i)   upon terms involving the issue, by any company, of debentures or other securities in respect of which a prospectus has been registered under the Companies Ordinance(Cap.32);

      (ii)   upon terms referable to the provision of property or services; or

      (iii)   by one company to another (neither company being an authorized institution) at a time when one is a subsidiary of the other or both are subsidiaries of another company, and references in this Ordinance to the taking or the making of a deposit shall be construed accordingly;

"depositor" means a person entitled to repayment of a deposit, whether made by him or not;

"Deposit-taking Companies Advisory Committee" means the Deposit-taking Companies Advisory Committee established by section 5;

"deposit-taking company" means a company which is currently registered;

"director" includes any person who occupies the position of director, whatever the title of his office;

"document" includes a circular, brochure, pamphlet, poster, handbill, prospectus and any other document which is directed at or likely to be read by members of the public; and also includes any newspaper, magazine, journal or other periodical publication;

"Exchange Fund" means the Exchange Fund established under the Exchange Fund Ordinance (Cap.66);

"exercise", in relation to a function, includes perform and discharge;

"former auditor" means a person who was formerly the auditor of an authorized institution or a former authorized institution;

"former authorized institution" means an institution which was formerly a bank, a restricted licence bank or a deposit-taking company;

"functions" includes powers and duties;

"holding company" and "subsidiary" have the same meaning as in the Companies Ordinance (Cap. 32);

"incorporated outside Hong Kong" includes established, by whatever means, outside Hong Kong;

"indirect controller", in relation to a company, means any person in accordance with whose directions or instructions the directors of the company or of another company of which it is a subsidiary are accustomed to act, but does not include a Manager or Advisor, or any person in accordance with whose directions or instructions those directors are accustomed to act by reason only that they act on advice given by him in his professional capacity;

"issue", in relation to an advertisement, invitation or document, includes publish, circulate, distribute or disseminate the advertisement, invitation or document; and also includes causing the advertisement, invitation or document to be issued;

"liquidity ratio" means the liquidity ratio referred to in section 102;

"local branch", in relation to-

    (a)   an authorized institution which is a bank, means-

        (i)   in the case of a bank incorporated in Hong Kong, a place of business thereof in Hong Kong, other than its principal place of business in Hong Kong, at which it carries on banking business; and

        (ii)   in the case of a bank incorporated outside Hong Kong, a place of business thereof in Hong Kong, other than its principal place of business in Hong Kong, at which it carries on banking business, but in either case does not mean an automated teller machine; and

    (b)   an authorized institution which is a deposit-taking company or a restricted licence bank, means a place of business in Hong Kong of a deposit-taking company or a restricted licence bank, other than its principal place of business in Hong Kong, at which it carries on the business of taking deposits;

"local representative office" means an office in Hong Kong of a bank within the meaning of section 46(9);

"majority shareholder controller", in relation to a company, means any person who, either alone or with any associate or associates, is entitled to exercise, or control the exercise of, more than 50% of the voting power at any general meeting of the company or of another company of which it is a subsidiary;

"Manager", in relation to an authorized institution, means the person appointed, pursuant to section 52(1)(C), to be the Manager of the institution;

"manager", in relation to an authorized institution, means its chief executive and any other person employed by the institution who, under the immediate authority of a director or of the chief executive, exercises managerial functions or is responsible for maintaining accounts or other records of the institution;

"minority shareholder controller", in relation to a company, means any person who, either alone or with any associate or associates, is entitled to exercise, or control the exercise of, 10% or more, but not more than 50%, of the voting power at any general meeting of the company or of another company of which it is a subsidiary;

"Monetary Authority" means the Monetary Authority appointed under section 5A of the Exchange Fund Ordinance (Cap.66);

"money at call" means money payable within not more than 24 hours of a demand therefor, but does not include money payable on demand;

"overseas branch" means a branch outside Hong Kong of an authorized institution incorporated in Hong Kong, at which it carries on banking business or a business of taking deposits, as the case may be, whether or not the business of the branch is limited by the laws or regulations of the place in which the branch is situated and whether or not the branch is referred to as an agency in such place;

"overseas representative office" means an office outside Hong Kong, other than an overseas branch, of an authorized institution incorporated in Hong Kong;

"register" means the register maintained under section 20;

"registered" means registered under section 16;

"reserves", in relation to an authorized institution, means reserves which appear in the accounts of the institution, but does not include any reserves which are represented by the writing down of the value of assets or by provision for the depreciation of fixed assets;

"restricted banking licence" means a restricted banking licence granted under section 16;

"restricted licence bank" means a company which holds a valid restricted banking licence;

"share" means share in the share capital of a company, and includes stock except where a distinction between stock or shares is expressed or implied; and the expression

"shareholder" includes a stockholder;

"short-term deposit" means a deposit with an original term to maturity of less than the period specified in item 1 of the First Schedule or with a period of call or notice of less than such specified period;

"specified sum", in relation to-

   (a)   a deposit-taking company, means the sum referred to in section 14(1)(a); and

   (b)   a restricted licence bank, means the sum referred to in section 14(1)(b);

"Unified Exchange" has the same meaning as in the Stock ExchangesUnification Ordinance (Cap. 361);

"unsuccessful", in relation to an appeal, includes any case where the appeal is abandoned or withdrawn;

"working day" means a day other than a public holiday or a gale warning day within the meaning of section 2 of the Judicial Proceedings (Adjournment During Gale Warning Days) Ordinance (Cap. 62).

(2)   For the purposes of this Ordinance-

   (a)   the taking of deposits includes holding out as being prepared to take deposits;

   (b)   an advertisement issued by any person by way of display or exhibition in a public place shall be treated as being issued by him on every day on which he causes or authorizes it to be displayed or exhibited;

   (c)   an advertisement or document which consists of or contains information likely to lead, directly or indirectly, members of the public to-

      (i)   make deposits; or

      (ii)   enter into, or offer to enter into, agreements to make deposits,

shall be treated as being an advertisement or document which is or contains an advertisement to members of the public so to do; and

      (d)   an advertisement or document issued by one person on behalf of or to the order of another shall be treated as an advertisement or document, as the case may be, issued by that other person.

(3) Without limiting the generality of any other meaning which "insolvent" may have, an authorized institution shall, for the purposes of this Ordinance, be deemed to be insolvent if it has ceased to pay its debts in the ordinary course of business or it cannot pay its debts as they become due.

(4) Where, under this Ordinance, an authorized institution is required to provide facilities to any person for the purpose of any investigation or examination of the institution, such facilities shall include photocopying facilities.

(5) Where there is any doubt or dispute as to whether a medium of exchange is a currency for the purposes of this Ordinance, the Monetary Authority may, by notice in the Gazette-

      (a)   declare that medium of exchange to be a currency for the purposes of this Ordinance;

      (b)   declare that medium of exchange not to be a currency for the purposes of this Ordinance.

(6) Any reference in this Ordinance to any person who signs any document includes a reference to any person who authorizes the signing of the document.

(7) Any reference in any provision of this Ordinance to a specified form means the form specified under section 133 for the purposes of that provision.

(8) For the avoidance of doubt, it is hereby declared that any reference in this Ordinance to taking a deposit (or words to the like effect) includes holding a deposit.

(9) Any reference in this Ordinance to the relevant banking supervisory authority, in relation to a company incorporated outside Hong Kong, means the banking supervisory authority outside Hong Kong which, in the opinion of the Monetary Authority, has primary supervisory responsibility for that company (and whether or not that authority is located in the place where that company is incorporated).

(10)   In sections 18(4), 22(4), 24(5) and 25(3), the term "continuing to hold a deposit" includes renewing a deposit.

Application

3.(1)   Part III of this Ordinance shall not apply to the taking of any deposit by -

(a)   a trust company registered under Part VIII of the Trustee Ordinance (Cap. 29);

(b)   a credit union registered under the Credit Unions Ordinance (Cap. 119);

(c)   a company, where such deposit is security by a mortgage, or charge, registered or to be registered under the Companies Ordinance (Cap. 32);

(d)   a person bona fide carrying on insurance business where such deposit is taken in the ordinary course of such business;

(e)   a person bona fide operating a superannuating or provident fund where such deposit is taken for the purposes of such fund;

(f)   a public utility company specified in Schedule 3 to the Inland Revenue Ordinance (Cap. 112) where such deposit is taken from a consumer;

(g)   an employer where such deposit is taken from a bona fide employee;

(h)   a solicitor, where such deposit is taken from a client, or as a stakeholder, in the ordinary course of his practice;

(i)   the Urban Council or the Regional Council;

(j)   a person who is a dealer within the meaning of the Securities Ordinance (Cap. 333) where section 84 of that Ordinance applies to such deposit, or a mutual fund corporation or unit trust authorized under section 15 of that Ordinance;

(k)   a person who is registered as a dealer under the Commodities Trading Ordinance (Cap. 250) where such deposit is taken from a client in the ordinary course of his business as a dealer;

(ka)   a person who is a licensed leveraged foreign exchange trader within the meaning of the Leveraged Foreign Exchange Trading

16

Ordinance (Cap. 451) where such deposit is taken from a client in the ordinary course of its business as a trader;

(l) a recognized clearing house within the meaning of section 2 of the Securities and Futures (Clearing Houses) Ordinance (Cap. 420), where such deposit is provided as security in relation to a market contract within the meaning of that section; or

(m) the Exchange Fund established by the Exchange Fund Ordinance (Cap.66).

(2) Part III of this Ordinance shall not apply to the taking of any deposit from-

(a) an authorized institution;

(b) a bank incorporated outside Hong Kong that is not an authorized institution;

(c) a money lender licensed under the Money Lenders Ordinance (Cap.163) in the ordinary course of his business as a money lender; or

(d) a pawnbroker licensed under the Pawnbrokers Ordinance (Cap. 166) in the ordinary course of his business as a pawnbroker.

(3) Notwithstanding anything in The HongKong and Shanghai Banking Corporation Limited Ordinance (Cap. 70), this Ordinance shall apply to The Hongkong and Shanghai Banking Corporation Limited.

(4) Where there is any conflict or inconsistency between this Ordinance and The Hongkong and Shanghai Banking Corporation Limited Ordinance (Cap.70) the provisions of this Ordinance shall prevail.

(5) An authorized institution which is incorporated or registered by or under the Companies Ordinance (Cap. 32) shall be subject to that Ordinance as well as to this Ordinance, except that where there is any conflict or inconsistency between this Ordinance and the Companies Ordinance (Cap. 32) the provisions of this Ordinance shall prevail.

PART II - Appointments, Functions Of Monetary Authority, Reports By
Monetary Authority And Power Of Governor To Give Directions

Banking Advisory Committee

4.(1) There is hereby established a Banking Advisory Committee for the purpose of advising the Governor upon any matter connected with this Ordinance, in particular in relation to banks and the carrying on of banking business, and of advising the Governor in Council in any case where the advice of the Committee is sought under section 53(2).

(2) The Banking Advisory Committee shall consist of the Financial Secretary, who shall be the chairman, the Monetary Authority, and such other persons, not being less than 4 nor more than 12, as the Governor may from time to time appoint.

(3) The members of the Banking Advisory Committee appointed by the Governor shall hold office for such period and upon such terms as theGovernor may specify in their appointments.

(4) In the absence of the chairman at any meeting of the Banking Advisory Committee, the Financial Secretary may appoint the chairman.

Deposit-taking Companies Advisory Committee

5.(1) There is hereby established a Deposit-taking Companies Advisory Committee for the purpose of advising the Governor upon any matter connected with this Ordinance, in particular in relation to deposit-taking companies and restricted licence banks and the carrying on of a business of taking deposits by them, and of advising the Governor in Council in any case where the advice of the Committee is sought under section 53(2).

(2) The Deposit-taking Companies Advisory Committee shall consist of the Financial Secretary, who shall be the chairman, the Monetary Authority, and such other persons, not being less than 4 nor more than 12, as the Governor may from time to time appoint.

(3) The members of the Deposit-taking Companies Advisory Committee appointed by the Governor shall hold office for such period and upon such terms as the Governor may specify in their appointments.

(4) In the absence of the chairman at any meeting of the Deposit-taking Companies Advisory Committee, the Financial Secretary may appoint the chairman.

6. (*Repealed*)

Functions of Monetary Authority

7.(1) The principal function of the Monetary Authority under this Ordinance shall be to promote the general stability and effective working of the banking system.

(2) Without limiting the generality of subsection (1), the Monetary Authority shall -

(a) be responsible for supervising compliance with the provisions of this Ordinance;

(b) take all reasonable steps to ensure that the principal places of business, local branches, overseas branches and overseas representative offices of all authorized institutions and local representative offices are operated in a responsible, honest and business-like manner;

(c) promote and encourage proper standards of conduct and sound and prudent business practices amongst authorized institutions;

(d) suppress or aid in suppressing illegal, dishonourable or improper practices in relation to the business practices of authorized institutions;

(e) co-operate with and assist recognized financial services supervisory authorities of Hong Kong or of any place outside Hong Kong, whenever appropriate, to the extent permitted by this or any other Ordinance; and

(f) consider and propose reforms of the law relating to banking business and the business of taking deposits.

(3) The Monetary Authority may from time to time cause to be prepared and published by notice in the Gazette, for the guidance of authorized institutions, guidelines not inconsistent with this Ordinance, indicating the manner in which he proposes to exercise functions conferred or imposed by this Ordinance upon him.

8. *(Repealed)*

Reports by Monetary Authority

9.(1) The Monetary Authority shall, as soon as practicable after each 31 December, prepare and furnish to the Financial Secretary a report on the working of this Ordinance and on the activities of his office during the preceding year and, in that report, may set out any measures that he considers necessary for improving the working of this Ordinance and of the activities of his office.

(2) In the report under subsection (1), the Monetary Authority shall draw attention to any breach or avoidance of this Ordinance that has come to his notice during the preceding year or any irregularity discovered by him in the accounts and records of the financial transactions of any authorized institution for that period which is, in his opinion, of sufficient importance to justify him so doing.

(3) The Monetary Authority shall, at such times as he considers necessary, report to the Financial Secretary on improvements that he considers to be desirable in the operation and management of his office.

(4) The Governor may, at any time, request the Monetary Authority to report to him on any matter relating to the working of this Ordinance or the activities of the office of the Monetary Authority, and the Monetary Authority shall, forthwith, prepare and furnish a report to the Governor accordingly.

(5) Where the Financial Secretary is furnished with a report under subsection (1), he may, as he thinks fit, publish the report, in whole or in part, in such manner as he thinks fit or decline to publish any part of the report.

(6) (*Repealed*)

Power of Governor to give directions

10.(1) The Governor may give to the Financial Secretary and the Monetary Authority such directions as he thinks fit with respect to the exercise of their respective functions under this Ordinance, either generally or in any particular case.

(2) The Financial Secretary and the Monetary Authority shall, in the exercise of their respective functions under this Ordinance, comply with any directions given by the Governor under this section.

PART III - Banking Business And Business Of Taking Deposits

To Be Carried On By Authorized Institutions Only

Banking business restricted to licensed banks

11.(1) No banking business shall be carried on in Hong Kong except by a bank (other than a bank the banking licence of which is for the time being suspended under section 24 or 25).

(2) Any person who and every director and every manager of a company which contravenes this section commits an offence and is liable-

> *(a)* on conviction upon indictment to a fine of $500,000 and to imprisonment for 5 years; or

> *(b)* on summary conviction to a fine of $50,000 and to imprisonment for 6 months.

Restriction on business of taking deposits

12.(1) No business of taking deposits shall be carried on in Hong Kong except by an authorized institution (other than an authorized institution the authorization of which is for the time being suspended under section 24 or 25).

(2) A deposit-taking company shall not take any short-term deposit in Hong Kong.

(3) A deposit-taking company shall not, without the written permission of the Monetary Authority, repay any deposit within a period of less than the period specified in item 1 of the First Schedule from the date on which the deposit was taken by the company.

(4) No deposit-taking company or restricted licence bank shall receive money on savings account.

(5) Subject to section 14, a restricted licence bank may take short-term deposits.

(6) Any person who contravenes subsection (1), every director and everymanager of a deposit-taking company which contravenes subsection (2), (3)or (4), and every director and every manager of a restricted licence bank which contravenes subsection (4), commits an offence and is liable-

> *(a)* on conviction upon indictment to a fine of $500,000 and to imprisonment for 5 years; or

> *(b)* on summary conviction to a fine of $50,000 and to imprisonment for 6 months.

(7) Any person who enters into a contract or arrangement, or uses any device or scheme, which has the effect of, or is designed to have the effect of, avoiding subsection (1), (2), (3) or (4) commits an offence and is liable-

> (a)   on conviction upon indictment to a fine of $500,000 and to imprisonment for 5 years; or

> (b)   on summary conviction to a fine of $50,000 and to imprisonment for 6 months.

(8) For the purposes of any proceedings for an offence under subsection (6), if it is proved that a person took deposits on at least 5 separate occasions within any period of 30 days, that person shall, in the absence of evidence to the contrary, be deemed to have been carrying on a business of taking deposits.

Power to grant exemptions

13.(1) The Financial Secretary may, by notice in the Gazette, exempt any person or class of persons from section 12(1) and, if the Financial Secretary thinks fit, in that notice also exempt that person or class of persons from section 92(1) in respect of the business of taking deposits to which the exemption from section 12(1) relates.

(2) An exemption under subsection (1) shall be subject to such conditions as are specified in the notice.

(3) The Financial Secretary may at any time by notice in the Gazette-

> (a)   revoke an exemption under subsection (1); or

> (b)   revoke, vary, or add to, any condition subject to which such exemption is granted.

Deposit-taking company not to take deposits less than specified sum

14.(1) Subject to subsection (2)-

> (a)   a deposit-taking company shall not take in Hong Kong any deposit from a depositor of a sum less than the amount specified in item 2 of the First Schedule; and

> (b)   a restricted licence bank shall not take in Hong Kong any deposit from a depositor of a sum less than the amount specified in item 3 of the First Schedule.

(2) A deposit-taking company or a restricted licence bank may take a deposit from a depositor of a sum less than the specified sum applying at the date of that deposit if the amount standing to the credit of the depositor with the deposit-taking company or restricted licence bank, as the case may be, at the time any such deposit is taken is not less than the specified sum applying at the date of that deposit.

(3) Except where a depositor withdraws the whole amount standing to his credit with a deposit-taking company or a restricted licence bank, the deposit-taking company or restricted licence bank, as the case may be, shall not at the time of the withdrawal of any sum permit the amount of the balance standing to the credit of the depositor to be less than the specified sum.

(4) Notwithstanding subsection (3), where a depositor has an amount standing to his credit with a deposit-taking company or a restricted licence bank at a time when the specified sum is amended by being increased, the deposit-taking company or restricted licence bank, as the case may be, may permit the amount of the balance to be reduced by withdrawals to any amount that is not less than the specified sum as it was before being so amended.

(5) Every director and every manager of a deposit-taking company or a restricted licence bank which contravenes subsection (1) or (3) commits an offence and is liable-

> *(a)*   on conviction upon indictment to a fine of $500,000 and to imprisonment for 2 years; or
>
> *(b)*   on summary conviction to a fine of $50,000 and to imprisonment for 6 months.

(6)   Any person who holds himself out, whether as a broker or agent of a deposit-taking company or a restricted licence bank or otherwise, as being prepared to take from any person, any sum less than the specified sum for the purpose of making a deposit of that sum, or of that sum and other sums, with the deposit-taking company or restricted licence bank, as the case may be, commits an offence and is liable-

> *(a)*   on conviction upon indictment to a fine of $500,000 and to imprisonment for 2 years; or
>
> *(b)*   on summary conviction to a fine of $50,000 and to imprisonment for 6 months.

(7)   Any person who enters into a contract or arrangement, or uses any device or scheme, which has the effect of, or is designed to have the effect of, avoiding subsection (1) or (3) commits an offence and is liable-

> *(a)*   on conviction upon indictment to a fine of $500,000 and to imprisonment for 5 years; or
>
> *(b)*   on summary conviction to a fine of $50,000 and to imprisonment for 6 months.

PART IV - Authorization

Application for authorization

15.(1) A company which proposes to carry on-

  (a) banking business;

  (b) a business of taking deposits as a deposit-taking company; or

  (c) a business of taking deposits as a restricted licence bank,

shall apply to the Monetary Authority for authorization to carry on that business.

(2) There shall be lodged with the Monetary Authority in respect of an application for authorization from a company-

  (a) a copy of the memorandum and articles of association or other document constituting the company, which shall be verified in such manner as the Monetary Authority may require; and

  (b) such other documents and information as may be required by the Monetary Authority.

Grant or refusal of authorization, etc.

16.(1) Subject to subsections (2) and (6), the Monetary Authority may, on receipt of an application in accordance with section 15 from a company-

  (a) authorize the company to carry on the business the subject of the application subject to such conditions, if any, as he may think proper to attach to the company's authorization in any particular case; or

  (b) refuse to so authorize the company.

(2) Without limiting the generality of subsection (1)(b), the Monetary Authority shall refuse to authorize a company under that subsection if any one or more of the criteria specified in the Seventh Schedule applicable to or in relation to the company are not fulfilled with respect to the company.

(3) The authorization of a company under subsection (1)(a) shall be effected by-

  (a) the grant of a banking licence where the carrying on of banking business is the subject of the company's application for authorization;

    (b)   registering the company where the carrying on of a business of taking deposits as a deposit-taking company is the subject of the company's application for authorization, for which purpose the Monetary Authority shall-

        (i)   enter in the register the relevant particulars specified in section 20; and

        (ii)   notify the company in writing of the registration and date of registration;

    (c)   the grant of a restricted banking licence where the carrying on of a business of taking deposits as a restricted licence bank is the subject of the company's application for authorization.

(4) Where the Monetary Authority refuses to authorize a company under subsection (1)(b), he shall notify the company in writing of-

    (a)   the refusal; and

    (b)   the reasons for the refusal.

(5) Without limiting the generality of subsection (1)(a) but subject to section 134A, the Monetary Authority may at any time, by notice in writing served on an authorized institution, attach to its authorization such conditions (including attach by way of amending conditions already attached to its authorization), or cancel any conditions attached to its authorization, as he may think proper.

(6) Before exercising his power under subsection (1)(b) to refuse to authorize a company, the Monetary Authority shall give the company an opportunity, within such period as the Monetary Authority may specify in writing, being a period reasonable in all the circumstances, of being heard.

(7) Any-

    (a)   company aggrieved by the refusal of the Monetary Authority to authorize it under subsection (1)(b); or

    (b)   authorized institution aggrieved by the attachment by the Monetary Authority of any conditions to its authorization under subsection (1)(a) or (5),

may appeal to the Governor in Council against the refusal or the conditions, but that refusal or those conditions, as the case may be, shall take effect immediately, notwithstanding that an appeal has been or may be made under this subsection.

(8) Every director and every manager of an authorized institution which contravenes any condition attached under subsection (1)(a) or (5) to its authorization commits an offence and is liable-

(a) on conviction upon indictment to a fine of $200,000; or

(b) on summary conviction to a fine of $50,000,and, in the case of a continuing offense, to a further fine of $5,000 for every day during which the offence continues.

(9) It is hereby declared that, without limiting the generality of subsection (1)(a) or (5), conditions attached under that subsection to an authorization may-

(a) impose restrictions, either generally or in any particular case, on the banking business, business of taking deposits as a deposit-taking company or business of taking deposits as a restricted licence bank, as the case may be, which may be carried on by the authorized institution to which the authorization relates;

(b) notwithstanding any other provisions of this Ordinance or the provisions of any other enactment (including the Companies Ordinance (Cap. 32)), impose requirements in relation to the accounts of the authorized institution to which the authorization relates, including-

(i) the institution's audited annual accounts within the meaning of section 60 (11);

(ii) any supplementary information to those audited annual accounts;

(iii) the report of the directors under section 129D(1) of the Companies Ordinance (Cap. 32);

(iv) the institution's cash flow statement, together with any notes thereon, where the statement does not already form part of those audited annual accounts;

(v) the disclosure (whether to the public or otherwise) of those audited annual accounts, that supplementary information, that report, that cash flow statement or those notes.

(10) The Monetary Authority may from time to time cause to be prepared and published by notice in the Gazette, for the guidance of companies seeking to be authorized, guidelines not inconsistent with this Ordinance, indicating the manner in which he proposes to exercise functions conferred or imposed by the Seventh Schedule upon him.

Application for authorization in the case of proposed company

17.   Where a body of persons proposes to form a company for the purpose of carrying on a business referred to in section 15(1), it may apply to the Monetary Authority for an intimation as to whether or not the company will be authorized to carry on that business upon its incorporation and, in the case of any such application, the provisions of sections 15(2) and 16 and the Seventh Schedule shall be read and have effect with such modifications as may be necessary to take account of such application.

Variation of authorization

18.(1) Where a deposit-taking company is authorized to carry on banking business or a business of taking deposits as a restricted licence bank, it shall thereupon cease to be a deposit-taking company.

(2) Where a restricted licence bank is authorized to carry on banking business or a business of taking deposits as a deposit-taking company, it shall thereupon cease to be a restricted licence bank.

(3) Where a bank is authorized to carry on a business of taking deposits as a deposit-taking company or as a restricted licence bank, it shall thereupon cease to be a bank.

(4) The Monetary Authority may, by notice in writing served on an authorized institution, consent to the institution continuing to hold a deposit-

> *(a)*   lawfully taken by the institution before the date on which subsection (1), (2) or (3) applied to the institution;

> *(b)*   the holding of which on or after that date would, but for this subsection, contravene any of the provisions of section 11, 12 or 14; and

> *(c)*   subject to such conditions, if any, as he may think proper to attach to the consent in any particular case,and, accordingly, if the institution continues to hold that deposit on or after that date pursuant to that consent and in accordance with those conditions, if any, then it shall be deemed not to have thereby contravened any of those provisions.

(5) Without limiting the generality of subsection (4)(c), the Monetary Authority may, by notice in writing served on an authorized institution, attach to a consent given to the institution pursuant to subsection (4) such conditions (including attach by way of amending conditions already attached to such consent), or cancel any conditions attached to such consent, as he may think proper.

(6) Without limiting the generality of subsection (4)(c) or (5), conditions referred to in that subsection may specify-

(a)   the period for which a deposit referred to in subsection (4) may be held by the authorized institution concerned;

(b)   the manner in which such deposit may be held or used by the institution.

(7) The Monetary Authority may, by notice in writing served on an authorized institution, require the institution to submit, within such period and in such manner as are specified in the notice, such information as he may reasonably require to ascertain whether the institution is complying with any conditions referred to in subsection (4)(c) or (5) attached to a consent given to the institution pursuant to subsection (4).

(8) Any authorized institution aggrieved by any conditions referred to in subsection (4)(c) or (5) attached to a consent given to the institution pursuant to subsection (4) may appeal against the conditions to the Governor in Council, but those conditions shall take effect immediately, notwithstanding that an appeal has been or may be made under this subsection.

(9) Every director and every manager of an authorized institution which contravenes any condition referred to in subsection (4)(c) or (5) attached to a consent given to the institution pursuant to subsection (4) commits an offence and is liable-

(a)   on conviction upon indictment to a fine of $200,000; or

(b)   on summary conviction to a fine of $50,000, and, in the case of a continuing offence, to a further fine of $5,000 for every day during which the offence continues.

(10)   Every director and every manager of an authorized institution which fails without reasonable excuse to comply with any requirement under subsection (7) commits an offense and is liable-

(a)   on conviction upon indictment to a fine of $200,000 and to imprisonment for 2 years and, in the case of a continuing offence, to a further fine of $10,000 for every day during which the offence continues; or

(b)   on summary conviction to a fine of $50,000 and to imprisonment for 6 months and, in the case of a continuing offence, to a further fine of $5,000 for every day during which the offence continues.

(11)   Any person who signs any document for the purposes of any requirement under subsection (7) which he knows or reasonably ought to know to be false in a material particular commits an offence and is liable-

(a)   on conviction upon indictment to a fine of $500,000 and to imprisonment for 2 years; or

(b)   on summary conviction to a fine of $50,000 and to imprisonment for 6 months.

Fees payable by authorized institutions

19.(1)   An authorized institution shall, within 14 days after the date on which it was authorized, pay to the Director of Accounting Services-

(a)   in the case of a bank, the banking licence fee;

(b)   in the case of a deposit-taking company, the registration fee;

(c)   in the case of a restricted licence bank, the restricted banking licence fee, specified in the Second Schedule.

(2)   Every authorized institution shall pay to the Director of Accounting Services annually-

(a)   in the case of a bank, the renewal of banking licence fee specified in the Second Schedule upon the anniversary of the date on which it was authorized;

(b)   in the case of a deposit-taking company, the renewal of registration fee specified in the Second Schedule-

    (i)   where the company was carrying on a business of taking deposits on 1 April 1976, on 1 April in each year;

    (ii)   where subparagraph (i) does not apply, upon the anniversary of the date on which it was authorized;

(c)   in the case of a restricted licence bank, the renewal of restricted banking licence fee specified in the Second Schedule upon the anniversary of the date on which it was authorized.

Register of authorized institutions, etc.

20.(1) The Monetary Authority shall maintain a register, in such form as he thinks fit, which shall contain-

(a)   the name and the address of the principal place of business in Hong Kong of every bank;

(b) the name of every bank which has a local representative office and the address of the place of business in Hong Kong of every local representative office;

(c) the name and the address of the principal place of business in Hong Kong of every deposit-taking company;

(d) the name and the address of the principal place of business in Hong Kong of every restricted licence bank;

(e) in the case of a bank (including a bank referred to in paragraph (b)), deposit-taking company or restricted licence bank, incorporated outside Hong Kong, the address of its principal place of business outside Hong Kong; and

(f) such other particulars of banks, local representative offices, deposit-taking companies or restricted licence banks as the Monetary Authority thinks fit (including particulars of any order of the High Court under section 53E(1)).

(2) The register shall be kept at the office of the Monetary Authority or at such other place as may be notified by the Monetary Authority in the Gazette.

(3) The Monetary Authority may require a bank, local representative office, deposit-taking company or restricted licence bank to submit such information for the purposes of subsection (1) as he may reasonably require in order to maintain the register in so far as it relates to that bank, local representative office, deposit-taking company or restricted licence bank, as the case may be, and such information shall be submitted within such period and in such manner as the Monetary Authority may require.

(4) Where any information submitted to the Monetary Authority under subsection (3) changes subsequent to the submission, the bank, local representative office, deposit-taking company or restricted licence bank which submitted the information shall give notice in writing to the Monetary Authority of such change not later than 21 days after such change takes place.

(5) Any member of the public may, with effect from such date and during such hours as shall be notified by the Monetary Authority in the Gazette, on payment of the fee specified in the Second Schedule-

(a) inspect the register or obtain a copy of an entry in the register or an extract from the register; or

(b) inspect or obtain a copy of or an extract from any document lodged with the Monetary Authority under section 15(2)(a).

(6) A document purporting to be-

    (a)   a copy of any entry in or extract from the register, or of any document lodged with the Monetary Authority by a company under this Ordinance; and

    (b)   signed and certified by the Monetary Authority as a true copy of the entry, extract or document referred to in paragraph (a), shall be admitted in evidence in criminal or civil proceedings before any court on its production without further proof, and-

        (i)   in the absence of evidence to the contrary, the court shall presume that-

            (A)   the signature and certification is that of the Monetary Authority; and

            (B)   the document is a true and correct copy of the entry, extract or document referred to in paragraph (a); and

        (ii)   such document shall be prima facie evidence of all matters contained therein.

(7) Every director and every manager of a bank, deposit-taking company or restricted licence bank, and any person in charge, or who appears to be in charge, of a local representative office, which fails, without reasonable excuse, to comply with a requirement under subsection (3), or to comply with subsection (4), commits an offence and is liable-

    (a)   on conviction upon indictment to a fine of $200,000 and to imprisonment for 2 years and, in the case of a continuing offence, to a further fine of $10,000 for every day during which the offence continues; or

    (b)   on summary conviction to a fine of $50,000 and to imprisonment for 6 months and, in the case of a continuing offence, to a further fine of $5,000 for every day during which the offence continues.

(8) If any bank, local representative office, deposit-taking company or restricted licence bank submits any information under subsection (3) or (4) which is false in a material particular, every director and every manager of the bank, deposit-taking company or restricted licence bank, or any person in charge, or who appears to be in charge, of the local representative office, as the case may be, commits an offence and is liable-

    (a)   on conviction upon indictment to a fine of $500,000 and to imprisonment for 2 years; or

(b)   on summary conviction to a fine of $50,000 and to imprisonment for 6 months.

Publication of names entered in or removed from register and suspensions

21.(1) Where the name of a bank (including a bank referred to in section 20(1)(b)), deposit-taking company or restricted licence bank is entered in the register, the Monetary Authority shall, as soon as reasonably practicable thereafter, publish in the Gazette notice of such entry.

(2) Where a company ceases to be a deposit-taking company, restricted licence bank or bank by virtue of section 18(1), (2) or (3) respectively, the Monetary Authority shall, as soon as reasonably practicable thereafter-

(a)   remove from the register the name of the former deposit taking company, restricted licence bank or bank, as the case may be; and

(b)   publish in the Gazette notice of such removal.

(3) Where the authorization of an authorized institution is revoked under this Ordinance, the Monetary Authority shall, as soon as reasonably practicable after the revocation takes effect-

(a)   remove from the register the name of the former authorized institution concerned; and

(b)   publish in the Gazette notice of such removal.

(4) Where the authorization of an authorized institution is suspended under section 24 or 25, the Monetary Authority shall, as soon as reasonably practicable thereafter-

(a)   make a notation in the register against the name of the authorized institution concerned that its authorization has been so suspended and, if such suspension is for a specified period, shall, in that notation, give particulars of such period; and

(b)   publish in the Gazette notice of such notation.

(5) Where approval for the establishment of a local representative office is revoked under this Ordinance, the Monetary Authority shall, as soon as reasonably practicable thereafter-

(a)   remove from the register the name of the bank which maintained the local representative office; and

(b)   publish in the Gazette notice of such removal.

PART V - Revocation Of Authorization

Revocation of authorization

22.(1) Subject to subsection (3) and section 23(1), the Monetary Authority may, after consultation with the Financial Secretary, propose to revoke the authorization of an authorized institution-

    (a)   on any one or more of the grounds specified in the Eighth Schedule applicable to or in relation to the institution; and

    (b)   by notice in writing served on the institution.

(2) Any authorized institution aggrieved by the proposed revocation of its authorization under subsection (1) may appeal to the Governor in Council against the proposed revocation.

(3) Where-

    (a)   an authorized institution serves a notice in writing on the Monetary Authority stating that it does not propose to appeal under subsection (2) against the proposed revocation of its authorization under subsection (1);

    (b)   the period specified in the Administrative Appeals Rules (Cap. 1 sub. leg.) within which an authorized institution may appeal under subsection (2) against the proposed revocation of its authorization under subsection (1) expires without any such appeal having been made; or

    (c)   an appeal under subsection (2) by an authorized institution against the proposed revocation of its authorization under subsection (1) is unsuccessful,the Monetary Authority shall, as soon as reasonably practicable thereafter, by notice in writing served on the institution, specify the date on and from which that revocation shall take effect (and, accordingly, that authorization shall be revoked on and from that date).

(4) The Monetary Authority may, by notice in writing served on an authorized institution (including a former authorized institution), consent to the institution continuing to hold a deposit-

    (a)   lawfully taken by the institution before the date on which the proposed revocation under subsection (1) of its authorization takes effect as specified in a notice under subsection (3) served on it;

(b)   the holding of which on or after that date would, but for this subsection, contravene any of the provisions of section 11, 12 or 23(2); and

(c)   subject to such conditions, if any, as he may think proper to attach to the consent in any particular case,

and, accordingly, if that institution continues to hold that deposit on or after that date pursuant to that consent and in accordance with those conditions, if any, then it shall be deemed not to have thereby contravened any of those provisions.

(5) Without limiting the generality of subsection (4)(c), the Monetary Authority may, by notice in writing served on an authorized institution (or former authorized institution), attach to a consent given to the institution pursuant to subsection (4) such conditions (including attach by way of amending conditions already attached to such consent), or cancel any conditions attached to such consent, as he may think proper.

(6) Without limiting the generality of subsection (4)(c) or (5), conditions referred to in that subsection may specify-

(a)   the period for which a deposit referred to in subsection (4) may be held by the authorized institution (or former authorized institution) concerned;

(b)   the manner in which such deposit may be held or used by the institution.

(7) The Monetary Authority may, by notice in writing served on an authorized institution (or former authorized institution), require the institution to submit, within such period and in such manner as are specified in the notice, such information as he may reasonably require in order to ascertain whether the institution will comply or is complying, as the case may be, with the conditions referred to in subsection (4)(c) or (5) attached to a consent given to the institution pursuant to subsection (4).

(8) Any authorized institution (or former authorized institution) aggrieved by any conditions referred to in subsection (4)(c) or (5) attached to a consent given to the institution pursuant to subsection (4) may appeal against the conditions to the Governor in Council, but those conditions shall take effect immediately, notwithstanding that an appeal has been or may be made under this subsection.

(9) Where the Monetary Authority serves a notice under subsection (3) on an authorized institution, he shall, as soon as reasonably practicable thereafter, publish in one English language newspaper (and in the English language) and one Chinese language newspaper (and in the Chinese language), each of which shall be a newspaper circulating in Hong Kong, a notice stating-

(a)   the name of the institution;

(b)   that the authorization of the institution has been revoked under this Ordinance; and

(c)   the date on and from which such revocation takes effect.

(10)   Every director and every manager of an authorized institution (or former authorized institution) which contravenes any condition referred to in subsection (4)(c) or (5) attached to a consent given to the institution pursuant to subsection (4) commits an offence and is liable-

(a)   on conviction upon indictment to a fine of $200,000; or

(b)   on summary conviction to a fine of $50,000, and, in the case of a continuing offence, to a further fine of $5,000 for every day during which the offence continues.

(11)   Every director and every manager of an authorized institution (or former authorized institution) which fails without reasonable excuse to comply with any requirement under subsection (7) commits an offence and is liable-

(a)   on conviction upon indictment to a fine of $200,000 and to imprisonment for 2 years and, in the case of a continuing offence, to a further fine of $10,000 for every day during which the offence continues; or

(b)   on summary conviction to a fine of $50,000 and to imprisonment for 6 months and, in the case of a continuing offence, to a further fine of $5,000 for every day during which the offence continues.

(12)   Any person who signs any document for the purposes of any requirement under subsection (7) which he knows or reasonably ought to know to be false in a material particular commits an offence and is liable-

(a)   on conviction upon indictment to a fine of $500,000 and to imprisonment for 2 years; or

(b)   on summary conviction to a fine of $50,000 and to imprisonment for 6 months.

Procedure on and effect of revocation of authorization

23.(1) The Monetary Authority shall, before exercising his power under section 22(1) to propose to revoke the authorization of an authorized institution, inform the institution of the ground or grounds for the proposed revocation and give it an opportunity, within such period as the Monetary Authority may specify in writing, being a period reasonable in all the circumstances, of being heard.

(2) Subject to section 22(4), immediately upon the proposed revocation of the authorization of an authorized institution taking effect in accordance with section 22(3), that institution shall cease to carry on the business the subject of its revoked authorization.

(3) Neither section 22(4) nor subsection (2) shall operate to prejudice the enforcement or other maintenance by any person of any right or interest against an authorized institution (or former authorized institution) referred to in that section or subsection, as the case may be, or by the institution of any right or interest against any person.

PART VI - Suspension Of Authorization

Temporary suspensions

24.(1) In any case where -

    (a)   the powers of the Monetary Authority become exercisable under section 22 (1) with respect to an authorized institution (and whether or not the Monetary Authority has complied with section 23(1) in respect of the institution); and

    (b)   the Monetary Authority-

        (i)   considers that it is necessary in the interests of depositors or potential depositors of the institution; or

        (ii)   is advised by the Financial Secretary that he considers that it is in the public interest, that urgent action be taken, he may, after consultation with the Financial Secretary-

    (i)   by notice in writing served on the institution suspend its authorization for a period not exceeding 14 days;

    (ii)   if he thinks fit, by reason of the urgency of the matter or otherwise, so suspend such authorization without giving the institution an opportunity of being heard.

(2) Any notice under subsection (1) may be accompanied by a notice stating that the Monetary Authority is considering whether to exercise his powers under section 22(1) or 25.

(3) Any accompanying notice referred to in subsection (2) shall inform the authorized institution concerned of its rights under sections 23(1) and 26 and the manner in which it may exercise such rights.

(4) Any suspension under this section or section 25 shall cease on such date prior to the expiration of the period thereof as the Monetary Authority may, by notice in writing served on the authorized institution the subject of the suspension, determine.

(5) The Monetary Authority may, by notice in writing served on an authorized institution, consent to the institution continuing to hold a deposit-

    (a)   lawfully taken by the institution before the date on which the suspension under subsection (1) of its authorization takes effect as specified in a notice under subsection (1) served on it;

    (b)   the holding of which on or after that date would, but for this subsection, contravene section 11, 12 or 27(1); and

    (c)   subject to such conditions, if any, as he may think proper to attach to the consent in any particular case,

and, accordingly, if that institution continues to hold that deposit on or after that date pursuant to that consent and in accordance with those conditions, if any, then it shall be deemed not to have thereby contravened that section.

(6) Without limiting the generality of subsection (5)(c), the Monetary Authority may, by notice in writing served on an authorized institution, attach to a consent given to the institution pursuant to subsection (5) such conditions (including attach by way of amending conditions already attached to such consent), or cancel any conditions attached to such consent, as he may think proper.

(7) Without limiting the generality of subsection (5)(c) or (6), conditions referred to in that subsection may specify-

    (a)   the period for which a deposit referred to in subsection (5) may be held by the authorized institution concerned;

    (b)   the manner in which such deposit may be held or used by the institution.

(8) The Monetary Authority may, by notice in writing served on anauthorized institution, require the institution to submit, within such period and in such manner as are specified in the notice, such information as he may reasonably require in order to ascertain whether the institution is complying with the conditions referred to in subsection (5)(c) or (6) attached to a consent given to the institution pursuant to subsection (5).

(9) Any authorized institution aggrieved by any conditions referred to insubsection (5)(c) or (6) attached to a consent given to the institution pursuant to subsection (5) may appeal against the conditions to the Governor in Council, but those conditions shall take effect immediately, notwithstanding that an appeal has been or may be made under this subsection.

(10)   Every director and every manager of an authorized institution which contravenes any condition referred to in subsection (5)(c) or (6) attached to a consent given to the institution pursuant to subsection (5) commits an offence and is liable-

    (a)   on conviction upon indictment to a fine of $200,000; or

    (b)   on summary conviction to a fine of $50,000,

and, in the case of a continuing offence, to a further fine of $5,000 for every day during which the offence continues.

(11) Every director and every manager of an authorized institution which fails without reasonable excuse to comply with any requirement under subsection (8) commits an offence and is liable-

        (a)   on conviction upon indictment to a fine of $200,000 and to imprisonment for 2 years and, in the case of a continuing offence, to a further fine of $ 10,000 for every day during which the offence continues; or

        (b)   on summary conviction to a fine of $50,000 and to imprisonment for 6 months and, in the case of a continuing offence, to a further fine of $5,000 for every day during which the offence continues.

(12) Any person who signs any document for the purposes of any requirement under subsection (8) which he knows or reasonably ought to know to be false in a material particular commits an offence and is liable-

        (a)   on conviction upon indictment to a fine of $500,000 and to imprisonment for 2 years; or

        (b)   on summary conviction to a fine of $50,000 and to imprisonment for 6 months.

Suspensions

25.(1) Subject to section 26, in any case where the powers of the Monetary Authority become exercisable under section 22(1) with respect to an authorized institution (and whether or not the Monetary Authority has complied with section 23(1) in respect of the institution), the Monetary Authority may, after consultation with the Financial Secretary, by notice in writing served on the institution, suspend its authorization for a period not exceeding 6 months.

(2) A suspension under this section may, before the expiration of the period thereof, be renewed by the Monetary Authority, after consultation with the Financial Secretary-

        (a)   by notice in writing served on the authorized institution the subject of the suspension; and

        (b)   for a period not exceeding 6 months commencing immediately upon the expiration of the suspension.

(3) The Monetary Authority may, by notice in writing served on an authorized institution, consent to the institution continuing to hold a deposit-

        (a)   lawfully taken by the institution before the date on which the

suspension under subsection (1) of its authorization takes effect as specified in a notice under that subsection served on it;

(b) the holding of which on or after that date would, but for this subsection, contravene section 11, 12 or 27(1); and

(c) subject to such conditions, if any, as he may think proper to attach to the consent in any particular case, and, accordingly, if that institution continues to hold that deposit on or after that date pursuant to that consent and in accordance with those conditions, if any, then it shall be deemed not to have thereby contravened that section.

(4) Without limiting the generality of subsection (3)(c), the Monetary Authority may, by notice in writing served on an authorized institution, attach to a consent given to the institution pursuant to subsection (3) such conditions (including attach by way of amending conditions already attached to such consent), or cancel any conditions attached to such consent, as he may think proper.

(5) Without limiting the generality of subsection (3)(c) or (4), conditions referred to in that subsection may specify

(a) the period for which a deposit referred to in subsection (3) may be held by the authorized institution concerned;

(b) the manner in which such deposit may be held or used by the institution.

(6) The Monetary Authority may, by notice in writing served on an authorized institution, require the institution to submit, within such period and in such manner as are specified in the notice, such information as he may reasonably require in order to ascertain whether the institution is complying with the conditions referred to in subsection (3)(c) or (4) attached to a consent given to the institution pursuant to subsection (3).

(7) Any authorized institution aggrieved by the suspension of its authorization under this section, or by any conditions referred to in subsection (3)(c) or (4) attached to a consent given to the institution pursuant to subsection (3), may appeal to the Governor in Council against the suspension or the conditions, as the case may be, but that suspension or those conditions, as the case may be, shall take effect immediately, notwithstanding that an appeal has been or may be made under this subsection.

(8) Every director and every manager of an authorized institution which contravenes any condition referred to in subsection (3)(c) or (4) attached to a consent given to the institution pursuant to subsection (3) commits an offence and is liable-

(a) on conviction upon indictment to a fine of $200,000; or

    (b)   on summary conviction to a fine of $50,000,

and, in the case of a continuing offence, to a further fine of $5,000 for every day during which the offence continues.

(9)   Every director and every manager of an authorized institution which fails without reasonable excuse to comply with any requirement under subsection (6) commits an offence and is liable-

    (a)   on conviction upon indictment to a fine of $200,000 and to imprisonment for 2 years and, in the case of a continuing offence, to a further fine of $10,000 for every day during which the offence continues; or

    (b)   on summary conviction to a fine of $50,000 and to imprisonment for 6 months and, in the case of a continuing offence, to a further fine of $5,000 for every day during which the offence continues.

(10)   Any person who signs any document for the purposes of any requirement under subsection (6) which he knows or reasonably ought to know to be false in a material particular commits an offence and is liable-

    (a)   on conviction upon indictment to a fine of $500,000 and to imprisonment for 2 years; or

    (b)   on summary conviction to a fine of $50,000 and to imprisonment for 6 months.

Opportunity of being heard

26.   The Monetary Authority shall, before exercising his powers under section 25, inform the authorized institution concerned of the ground or grounds therefor and give it an opportunity, within such period as the Monetary Authority may specify in writing, being a period reasonable in all the circumstances, of being heard.

Effect of suspension

27.(1) Without prejudice to any other provision of this Ordinance, where the authorization of an authorized institution is suspended under section 24 or 25, the institution shall, on and from the date specified in the notification to it by the Monetary Authority of such suspension, cease to carry on the business the subject of its authorization unless and until the period of suspension is terminated without revocation of that authorization and without a further period of suspension under this Part.

(2)   Notwithstanding the suspension under section 24 or 25 of the authorization of an authorized institution, the institution shall, unless otherwise specified in the notice concerned under that section served on the institution, during the period of its suspension, continue to be an authorized institution for the purposes of-

(a)   section 19;

(b)   Parts VIII, IX and X;

(c)   all the duties imposed on a bank, deposit-taking company or restricted licence bank, as the case may be, under this Ordinance.

(3)   Sections 24(5) and 25(3) and this section shall not operate to prejudice the enforcement or other maintenance by any person of any right or interest against an authorized institution referred to in subsection (1) or by the institution of any right or interest against any person.

PART VII - Transfer Of Authorization

Transfer of authorization

28.(1) Subject to this Ordinance, the authorization of an authorized institution may be transferred from that institution to another person.

(2) A transfer of the authorization of an authorized institution shall not take effect until the Monetary Authority grants the transfer or until such later date as the Monetary Authority specifies.

Application for transfer

29.(1) The person to whom it is proposed to transfer the authorization of an authorized institution shall lodge an application for the transfer of the authorization with the Monetary Authority.

(2 Subject to such modifications as may be necessary, sections 15, 16, 17 and 19 and the Seventh Schedule shall apply to an application for the transfer of the authorization of an authorized institution as if that application were an application for authorization under section 15(1).

Certificate of transfer, etc.

30. Where the Monetary Authority grants the transfer of the authorization of an authorized institution, he shall-

    (a)   issue a certificate of transfer to the applicant; and

    (b)   comply with such provisions of section 21 in respect of the transfer of the authorization as he may think appropriate.

Liabilities and privileges of transferer and transferee

31. Upon the issue of a certificate of transfer under section 30-

    (a)   the applicant shall have and may exercise the same privileges, and be subject to the same liabilities and penalties, under this Ordinance as if the authorization transferred had been originally granted to the applicant; and

    (b)   the person whose authorization is transferred shall cease to be authorized, but the transfer shall not affect the liability of that or any other person for any act or omission done, caused, permitted or made prior to the transfer.

32-43. *(Repealed)*

PART VIII - Local Branches, Local Representative Offices And Fees

Control of establishment, etc. of local branches

44.(1) An authorized institution shall not establish or maintain any local branch thereof without the approval of the Monetary Authority.

(2) Subsection (1) applies to every authorized institution whether the institution was authorized before, on or after the commencement of this Ordinance, and subsections (4) and (5) apply to an approval granted under subsection (1) whether the approval was granted before, on or after such commencement.

(3) Approval under subsection (1) shall be deemed to have been granted in respect of any local branch lawfully established prior to the commencement of this Ordinance.

(4) The Monetary Authority may at any time, by notice in writing served upon an authorized institution, attach to an approval granted under subsection (1), or deemed to have been granted under subsection (3), in respect of any local branch thereof such conditions, or amend or cancel any conditions so attached, as he may think proper.

(5) The Monetary Authority may at any time revoke, in such case as he thinks fit, an approval granted under subsection (1), or deemed to have been granted under subsection (3), in respect of any local branch.

(6) Where the Monetary Authority refuses to grant approval under subsection (1) or revokes an approval under subsection (5), he shall notify the authorized institution concerned in writing of the refusal or revocation.

(7) Any authorized institution aggrieved by the refusal to grant approval under subsection (1) or by the revocation of an approval under subsection (5) by the Monetary Authority, or by any conditions to which an approval is made subject by the Monetary Authority under subsection (4), may appeal to the Governor in Council against the refusal, the revocation or the conditions, but that refusal, that revocation or, as the case may be, those conditions shall take effect immediately, notwithstanding that an appeal has been or may be made under this subsection.

(8) Every director and every manager of an authorized institution which contravenes subsection (1) or any condition attached under subsection (4) commits an offence and is liable-

  (a)   on conviction upon indictment to a fine of $200,000; or

  (b)   on summary conviction to a fine of $50,000, and, in the case of a continuing offence, to a further fine of $5,000 for every day during which the offence continues.

Fees in respect of local branches

45.(1) Where the establishment by an authorized institution of a local branch is approved under section 44, the institution shall pay to the Director of Accounting Services the fee specified in the Second Schedule in relation to that branch and thereafter, so long as the branch continues to be maintained by the institution, it shall pay to the Director of Accounting Services the fee specified in the Second Schedule on the anniversary in each year of the date on which the institution was authorized.

(2) An authorized institution that is maintaining, at the commencement of this Ordinance, a local branch to which section 44(3) applies shall, so long as the branch continues to be maintained by the institution, pay to the Director of Accounting Services the fee specified in the Second Schedule on the anniversary in each year of the date on which the institution was authorized.

Control of establishment, etc. of local representative offices

46.(1) A bank shall not establish or maintain any local representative office thereof without the approval of the Monetary Authority.

(2) Approval under subsection (1) shall be deemed to have been granted in respect of any local representative office lawfully established prior to the commencement of the Banking (Amendment) Ordinance 1993 (94 of 1993).

(3) Approval under subsection (1) shall not be granted unless theMonetary Authority is satisfied that the bank is adequately supervised by therelevant banking supervisory authority.

(4) The Monetary Authority may at any time, by notice in writing served upon a bank, attach to an approval granted under subsection (1), or deemed to have been granted under subsection (2), in respect of any local representative office thereof such conditions, or amend or cancel any conditions so attached, as he may think proper.

(5) The Monetary Authority may at any time revoke, in such case as he thinks fit, an approval granted under subsection (1), or deemed to have been granted under subsection (2), in respect of any local representative office.

(6) Where the Monetary Authority refuses to grant approval under subsection (1) or revokes an approval under subsection (5), he shall notify the bank concerned in writing of the refusal or revocation.

(7) Any bank aggrieved by the refusal to grant approval under subsection(1) or by the revocation of an approval under subsection (5) by the Monetary Authority, or by any conditions to which an approval is made subject by the Monetary Authority under subsection (4), may appeal to the Governor in Council against the refusal, the revocation or the conditions, but that refusal, that revocation or, as the case may be, those conditions shall take effect immediately, notwithstanding that an appeal has been or may be made under this subsection.

(8) Any person in charge, or who appears to be in charge, of a local representative office established or maintained in contravention of subsection (1) or in respect of which any condition attached under subsection (4) is contravened, commits an offence and is liable-

(a) on conviction upon indictment to a fine of $200,000; or

(b) on summary conviction to a fine of $50,000,and, in the case of a continuing offence, to a further fine of $5,000 for every day during which the offence continues.

(9) In this section, "bank" means a company incorporated outside HongKong which-

(a) is neither an authorized institution nor recognized as the central bank of the place in which it is incorporated; and

(b) may, whether or not in or outside the place where it is incorporated, lawfully take deposits from the general public, whether or not on current account.

Supply of information and examination of local representative offices

47.(1) A bank which maintains a local representative office thereof pursuant to section 46 shall -

(a) submit to the Monetary Authority such information as he may require regarding the functions and activities of the representative office;

(b) if the Monetary Authority wishes to examine the functions and activities of the representative office, for that purpose afford to the person carrying out the examination access to the documents maintained by the representative office and to such information and facilities as may be required to conduct the examination, and shall produce to the person carrying out the examination such documents or other information as he may require.

(2) Any person who fails to comply with any requirement of theMonetary Authority under this section commits an offence and is liable-

(a) on conviction upon indictment to a fine of $200,000; or

(b) on summary conviction to a fine of $50,000,and, in the case of a continuing offence, to a further fine of $5,000 for every day during which the offence continues.

(3) Any person who signs any document for the purposes of this section which he knows or reasonably ought to know to be false in a material particular commits an offence and is liable -

(a)   on conviction upon indictment to a fine of $500,000 and to imprisonment for 2 years; or

(b)   on summary conviction to a fine of $50,000 and to imprisonment for 6 months.

(4) If a bank produces any book, account, document, security or information whatsoever under this section which is false in a material particular, every director and every manager of the bank commits an offence and is liable-

(a)   on conviction upon indictment to a fine of $500,000 and to imprisonment for 2 years; or

(b)   on summary conviction to a fine of $50,000 and to imprisonment for 6 months.

Fees in respect of local representative offices

48.(1)   Where the establishment by a bank of a local representative office is approved under section 46(1), the bank shall pay to the Director of Accounting Services the fee specified in the Second Schedule in relation to that representative office and thereafter, so long as the representative office continues to be maintained by the bank, the bank shall pay to the Director of Accounting Services the fee specified in the Second Schedule on the anniversary in each year of the date of the grant of the approval under that section.

(2) A bank that is maintaining, at the commencement of the Banking (Amendment) Ordinance 1993 (94 of 1993), a local representative office to which section 46(2) applies and which representative office was established prior to 1 April 1982 shall, so long as the representative office continues to be maintained by the bank, pay to the Director of Accounting Services the fee specified in the Second Schedule on 1 April of each year.

(3) A bank that is maintaining, at the commencement of the Banking (Amendment) Ordinance 1993 (94 of 1993), a local representative office to which section 46(2) applies and which representative office was established on or after 1 April 1982 shall, so long as the representative office continues to be maintained by the bank, pay to the Director of Accounting Services the fee specified in the Second Schedule on the anniversary in each year of the date of the grant of approval, under section 12C(1) of the Banking Ordinance 1964 (Cap. 155, 1983 Ed.) repealed by this Ordinance, of the establishment of that local representative office.

PART IX - Overseas Branches, Overseas Representative Offices, Fees And

Overseas Banking Corporations

Control of establishment, etc. of overseas branches

and overseas representative offices

49.(1) Without prejudice to section 44, an authorized institution which is incorporated in Hong Kong shall be subject to a condition that the institution shall not establish or maintain any overseas branch or overseas representative office thereof without the approval of the Monetary Authority.

(2) Subsection (1) applies to every authorized institution incorporated in Hong Kong whether the institution was authorized before, on or after the commencement of this Ordinance, and subsections (4) and (5) apply to an approval granted under subsection (1) whether the approval was granted before, on or after such commencement.

(3) Approval under subsection (1) shall be deemed to have been granted in respect of any overseas branch or overseas representative office lawfully established prior to the commencement of this Ordinance.

(4) The Monetary Authority may at any time, by notice in writing served upon an authorized institution, attach to an approval granted under subsection (1), or deemed to have been granted under subsection (3), in respect of anyoverseas branch or overseas representative office thereof such conditions, or amend or cancel any conditions so attached, as he may think proper.

(5) The Monetary Authority may at any time revoke, in such case as hethinks fit, an approval granted under subsection (1), or deemed to have been granted under subsection (3), in respect of any overseas branch or overseas representative office.

(6) Where the Monetary Authority refuses to grant approval under subsection (1) or revokes an approval under subsection (5), he shall notify the authorized institution concerned in writing of the refusal or revocation.

(7) Any authorized institution aggrieved by the refusal to grant approval under subsection (1) or by the revocation of an approval under subsection (5) by the Monetary Authority, or by any conditions to which an approval is made subject by the Monetary Authority under subsection (4), may appeal to the Governor in Council against the refusal, the revocation or the conditions, but that refusal, that revocation or, as the case may be, those conditions shall take effect immediately, notwithstanding that an appeal has been or may be made under this subsection.

(8) Every director and every manager of an authorized institution which contravenes the condition in subsection (1) or any condition attached under subsection (4) commits an offence and is liable-

        (a)   on conviction upon indictment to a fine of $200,000; or

(b)   on summary conviction to a fine of $50,000,

and, in the case of a continuing offence, to a further fine of $5,000 for every day during which the offence continues.

Conditions regarding overseas branches and overseas representative offices

50.(1) Every authorized institution incorporated in Hong Kong whichmaintains an overseas branch thereof shall be subject to a condition that-

(a)   the institution shall submit to the Monetary Authority a return in such form, and at such intervals, as he may specify showing the assets and liabilities of the overseas branch;

(b)   the institution shall submit to the Monetary Authority such further information as he may consider necessary for the proper understanding of the functions and activities of the overseas branch, and that such information shall be submitted within such period and in such manner as the Monetary Authority may require;

(c)   if the Monetary Authority requires any return submitted to him pursuant to paragraph (a), or any information submitted to him pursuant to a requirement under paragraph (b), to be accompanied by a report prepared by, subject to subsection (2A), an auditor or auditors appointed by the institution, the institution shall submit a report as to whether or not, in the opinion of the auditor or auditors, the return or information is correctly compiled, in all material respects, from the books and records of the overseas branch;

(d)   if the Monetary Authority wishes to examine the books, accounts and transactions of the overseas branch, the institution shall for that purpose afford the person carrying out the examination at the place where the branch is maintained access to the books and accounts of the branch, to documents of title to the assets and other documents and to all securities held by the branch in respect of its customers' transactions and its cash and to such information and facilities as may be required to conduct the examination, and that the institution shall produce to the person carrying out the examination such books, accounts, documents, securities, cash or other information as he may require:

Provided that, so far as is consistent with the conduct of the examination, such books, accounts, documents, securities and cash shall not be required to be produced at such times and such places as shall interfere with the proper conduct of the normal daily business of the overseas branch.

(2) Every authorized institution incorporated in Hong Kong which maintains an overseas representative office thereof shall be subject to a condition that-

> *(a)* the institution shall submit to the Monetary Authority such information as he may require regarding the functions and activities of the overseas representative office;

> *(b)* if the Monetary Authority wishes to examine the functions and activities of the overseas representative office, the institution shall for that purpose afford the person carrying out the examination at the place where the representative office is maintained access to the documents maintained by the representative office and to such information and facilities as may be required to conduct the examination, and that the institution shall produce to the person carrying out the examination such documents or other information as he may require.

(2A) The auditor or auditors appointed by an authorized institution to prepare a report required under subsection (1)(c) shall be-

> *(a)* an auditor or auditors appointed by the institution prior to the report being so required and approved by the Monetary Authority for the purpose of preparing the report;

> *(b)* an auditor approved, or an auditor from amongst auditors nominated, by the Monetary Authority for the purpose of preparing the report after consultation with the institution; or

> *(c)* an auditor referred to in paragraph (a) and an auditor referred to in paragraph (b), as may be required by the Monetary Authority.

(3) This section applies to every authorized institution incorporated in Hong Kong whether the institution was authorized before, on or after the commencement of this Ordinance.

(4) Every director and every manager of an authorized institution which contravenes any condition in subsection (1) or (2), or fails to comply with any requirement under those subsections, commits an offence and is liable-

> *(a)* on conviction upon indictment to a fine of $200,000 and to imprisonment for 12 months; or

(b)   on summary conviction to a fine of $50,000 and to imprisonment for 6 months,

and, in the case of a continuing offence, to a further fine of $5,000 for every day during which the offence continues.

(5) If an authorized institution produces any book, account, document, security or information whatsoever under this section which is false in a material particular, every director and every manager of the institution commits an offence and is liable-

(a)   on conviction upon indictment to a fine of $500,000 and to imprisonment for 2 years; or

(b)   on summary conviction to a fine of $50,000 and to imprisonment for 6 months.

(6) Any person who signs any document for the purposes of this section which he knows or reasonably ought to know to be false in a material particular commits an offence and is liable-

(a)   on conviction upon indictment to a fine of $500,000 and to imprisonment for 2 years; or

(b)   on summary conviction to a fine of $50,000 and to imprisonment for 6 months.

Fees in respect of overseas branches and overseas representative offices

51.(1) Whenever the establishment by an authorized institution incorporated in Hong Kong of an overseas branch or overseas representative office is approved under section 49(1), the institution shall pay to the Director of Accounting Services the fee specified in the Second Schedule in relation to that branch or representative office and thereafter, so long as the branch or representative office continues to be maintained by the institution, it shall pay to the Director of Accounting Services the fee specified in the Second Schedule on the anniversary in each year of the date on which the institution was authorized.

(2)   An authorized institution incorporated in Hong Kong that is maintaining, at the commencement of this Ordinance, an overseas branch or overseas representative office to which section 49(3) applies shall, so long as the branch or representative office continues to be maintained by the institution, pay to the Director of Accounting Services the fee specified in the Second Schedule on the anniversary in each year of the date on which the institution was authorized.

Control of establishment, etc. of overseas banking corporations

51A.(1) In this section-

"overseas banking corporation" means a company which-

(a)   is incorporated outside Hong Kong (and whether or not it is an authorized institution); and

(b)   may, whether or not in or outside Hong Kong, lawfully take deposits from the general public, whether or not on current account;

"relevant day" means the day of commencement of the Banking (Amendment) Ordinance 1993 (94 of 1993

(2) An authorized institution incorporated in Hong Kong, and any holding company incorporated in Hong Kong of such an institution, shall each be subject to a condition that it shall not-

(a)   establish or acquire, by whatever means, an overseas banking corporation such that that corporation becomes the subsidiary of the institution or of the holding company, as the case may be, without the approval of the Monetary Authority;

(b)   if any such approval granted in respect of that corporation is revoked under subsection (5), maintain that corporation as a subsidiary on or after the time such revocation comes into effect.

(3) Approval under subsection (2) shall be deemed to have been granted in respect of any overseas banking corporation-

(a)   which was, immediately before the relevant day, the subsidiary of an authorized institution or of any holding company of the institution; or

(b)   which becomes, not later than 3 months after the relevant day, the subsidiary of an authorized institution or of any holding company of the institution where the acts or circumstances by virtue of which such corporation became such a subsidiary substantially occurred before the relevant day.

(4) The Monetary Authority may at any time, by notice in writing served upon an authorized institution or its holding company, attach to an approval granted under subsection (2), or deemed to have been granted under subsection (3), in respect of any overseas banking corporation which is to become or is a subsidiary of the institution or of the holding company, as the case may be, such conditions, or amend or cancel any conditions so attached, as he may think proper.

(5)   The Monetary Authority may revoke-

>   *(a)*   in such case as he thinks fit; and

>   *(b)*   with effect from such time as is specified by him, being a time reasonable in all the circumstances of such case,

an approval granted under subsection (2), or deemed to have been granted under subsection (3), in respect of any overseas banking corporation.

(6) Where the Monetary Authority refuses to grant approval under subsection (2) or revokes an approval under subsection (5), he shall notify the authorized institution or its holding company concerned in writing of the refusal or revocation.

(7) Any authorized institution or its holding company aggrieved by the refusal to grant approval under subsection (2) or by the revocation of an approval under subsection (5) by the Monetary Authority, or by any conditions to which an approval is made subject by the Monetary Authority under subsection (4), may appeal to the Governor in Council against the refusal, the revocation or the conditions, but that refusal, that revocation or, as the case may be, those conditions shall take effect immediately, notwithstanding that an appeal has been or may be made under this subsection.

(8) Every director and every manager of an authorized institution or of its holding company which contravenes the condition in subsection (2) or any condition attached under subsection (4) commits an offence and is liable-

>   *(a)*   on conviction upon indictment to a fine of $200,000; or

>   *(b)*   on summary conviction to a fine of $50,000,

and, in the case of a continuing offence, to a further fine of $5,000 for every day during which the offense continues.

PART X - Powers Of Control Over Authorized Institutions

Powers of Monetary Authority

52.(1) Where-

- *(a)* an authorized institution informs the Monetary Authority-

  - **(i)** that it is likely to become unable to meet its obligations; or

  - **(ii)** that it is insolvent or about to suspend payment;

- *(b)* an authorized institution becomes unable to meet its obligations or suspends payment;

- *(c)* after an examination or investigation is made under section 55, or a report required under section 59(2) or 63(3A) is submitted, the Monetary Authority is of the opinion that an authorized institution-

  - **(i)** is carrying on its business in a manner detrimental to the interests of its depositors or potential depositors or of its creditors;

  - **(ii)** is insolvent or is likely to become unable to meet its obligations or is about to suspend payment;

  - **(iii)** has contravened or failed to comply with any of the provisions of this Ordinance; or

  - **(iv)** has contravened or failed to comply with any condition attached under section 16 to its authorization, the condition specified in section 49(1), the condition specified in section 50(1), the condition specified in section 50(2) or the condition specified in section 51A(2); or

- *(d)* the Financial Secretary advises the Monetary Authority that he considers it in the public interest to do so, #

the Monetary Authority, after consultation with the Financial Secretary, may exercise such one or more of the following powers as may from time to time appear to him to be necessary-

- *(A)* to require the institution, by notice in writing served on it, forthwith to take any action or to do any act or thing whatsoever in relation to its affairs, business and property as he may consider necessary (including any requirement imposing restrictions on the banking business, business of taking deposits as a deposit-taking company or business of taking deposits as a restricted licence bank, as the case may be, which may be carried on by the institution);

(B)   subject to subsection (3E), to give a direction that, during the period for which the direction is in force, the institution shall seek advice on the management of its affairs, business and property from an Advisor, for which purpose the Monetary Authority shall appoint a person to be the Advisor of that institution;

(C)   subject to subsections (3D) and (3E), to give a direction that, during the period for which the direction is in force, such of the affairs, business and property of the institution as are specified in the direction shall be managed by a Manager, for which purpose the Monetary Authority shall-

  (I)   appoint a person to be the Manager of that institution; and

  (II)   specify in the direction the primary objective or objectives (not inconsistent with the provisions of this Ordinance) with which the Manager shall comply;

(D)   to report the circumstances to the Governor in Council.

(2)   Except in the circumstances specified in subsection (1)(a), the Monetary Authority shall not exercise the power conferred by subsection (1)(D) unless he has-

  (a)   where the authorized institution is incorporated in Hong Kong and a direction given under subsection (1)(C) is in force in respect of the institution-

    (i)   given to the institution, and such relevant persons, if any, as he thinks fit, not less than 7 days' notice in writing (or such lesser period as is permitted under subsection (2A)) stating-

      (A)   his intention to exercise such power; and

                (B)   his reasons for the exercise thereof; and

        (ii)   afforded the institution, and such relevant persons, if any, as he thinks fit, an opportunity to submit to him representations in writing thereon (which representations, if any, shall form part of his report to the Governor in Council);

  (b)   where the authorized institution is incorporated outside Hong Kong and a direction given under subsection (1)(C) is in force in respect of the institution-

        (i)   given to the institution, at its principal place of business outside Hong Kong, not less than 7 days' notice in writing (or such lesser period as is permitted under subsection (2A)) stating-

                (A)   his intention to exercise such power; and

                (B)   his reasons for the exercise thereof; and

        (ii)   afforded the institution an opportunity to submit to him representations in writing thereon (which representations, if any, shall form part of his report to the Governor in Council);

  (c)   in any other case-

        (i)   given to the authorized institution not less than 7 days' notice in writing (or such lesser period as is permitted under subsection (2A)) stating-

                (A)   his intention to exercise such power; and

                (B)   his reasons for the exercise thereof; and

        (ii)   afforded the institution an opportunity to submit to him representations in writing thereon (which representations, if any, shall form part of his report to the Governor in Council).

(2A)   The Monetary Authority may give an authorized institution and any relevant person less than the 7 days' notice in writing referred to in subsection (2 where-

  (a)   he has the consent of the Financial Secretary to do so; and

        (b)   to do so is reasonable in the circumstances.

(3)   *(Repealed)*

(3A)   Subject to subsection (3D), the Monetary Authority may from time to time vary a direction given under subsection (1)(C) in respect of-

        (a)   the affairs, business and property specified in the direction of the authorized institution to which the direction relates;

        (b)   the primary objective or objectives specified in the direction with which the Manager of the institution shall comply.

(3B)   It is hereby declared that any thing done, in reliance on a direction given under subsection (1)(C), at any time before a variation under subsection (3A) of that direction shall not be invalid by reason only of that variation.

(3C)   During the period for which a direction given under subsection (1)(C) is in force in respect of an authorized institution, any reference in this Part to -

        (a)   the affairs, business or property, or any combination thereof, of the institution; or

        (b)   the primary objective or objectives with which the Manager of the institution shall comply,

shall, unless the context otherwise requires, be construed to mean-

        (i)   where paragraph (a) is applicable, such affairs, business or property, or combination thereof, as the case may be;

        (ii)   where paragraph (b) is applicable, such primary objective or objectives,

specified in that direction as varied from time to time under subsection (3A).

(3D)   Notwithstanding any other provision of this Part, no direction given under subsection (1)(C) (including any variation thereof under subsection (3A)) in respect of an authorized institution incorporated outside Hong Kong shall apply to any of the affairs, business or property of the institution except-

        (a)   so much of the affairs and business of the institution as are carried on, or managed, in or from Hong Kong; and

(b)   so much of the property of the institution as is either or both of the following-

    (i)   located in, or managed from, Hong Kong;

    (ii)   an asset of the institution's principal place of business in Hong Kong or of any local branch.

(3E)   The Monetary Authority shall not give a direction under subsection (1)(B) or

C)   in respect of an authorized institution in relation to which the High Court has made an order for the winding-up of the institution.

(3F)   It is hereby declared that the Monetary Authority may exercise his power under subsection (1)(B) or (C) in such a way as to appoint -

(a)   a company or partnership; or

(b)   without prejudice to the generality of paragraph (a), 2 or more persons, to be the Advisor or Manager, as the case may be, of an authorized institution.

(3G)   Where the Monetary Authority exercises his power under subsection (1)(C) in such a way as to appoint 2 or more persons to be the Manager of an authorized institution, he shall-

(a)   by notice in writing, specify which of the duties and powers imposed or conferred on a Manager under this Ordinance shall be discharged or exercised, as the case may be, in relation to the institution, by-

    (i)   any such person alone;

    (ii)   any such persons jointly;

    (iii)   each such person; and

(b)   attach that notice to the direction concerned given under that subsection served on the institution under section 53A(1),

and the provisions of this Ordinance (including section 53G) shall be read and have effect with such modifications as are necessary to take into account that notice.

(3H)   For the avoidance of doubt, it is hereby declared that a person appointed under subsection (1)(B) or (C) to be the Advisor or Manager of an authorized institution may be a person who holds an appointment under section 5A(3) of the Exchange Fund Ordinance (Cap. 66).

(3I)   Any person aggrieved by the exercise by the Monetary Authority of any power conferred on him by subsection (1)(A), (B) or (C) or (3A) may appeal to the Governor in Council against the exercise of that power, but the exercise of that power shall take effect immediately, notwithstanding that an appeal has been or may be made under this subsection.

(4)   Every director and every manager of an authorized institution which fails to comply with any requirement of the Monetary Authority under subsection (1)(A) commits an offence and is liable-

> *(a)*   on conviction upon indictment to a fine of $1,000,000 and to imprisonment for 5 years and, in the case of a continuing offence, to a further fine of $50,000 for every day during which the offence continues; or

> *(b)*   on summary conviction to a fine of $50,000 and to imprisonment for 2 years and, in the case of a continuing offence, to a further fine of $5,000 for every day during which the offence continues.

(5)   In this section, "relevant person", in relation to an authorized institution, means any person who-

> *(a)*   is the Manager of the institution;

> *(b)*   is a minority shareholder controller, majority shareholder controller or indirect controller of the institution;

> *(c)*   has ceased to be a chief executive or director of the institution by virtue of section 53B(1)(a);

> *(d)*   is a chief executive or director of the institution by virtue of the operation of section 53B(2).

Powers of Governor in Council

53.(1) Where-

> *(a)*   the Monetary Authority makes a report to the Governor in Council under section 52(1)(D);

> *(b)*   any person appeals to the Governor in Council under section 52(3I); or

> *(c)*   the Financial Secretary refers a report and his recommendations thereon to the Governor in Council under section 117(5)(c),

the Governor in Council may, without prejudice to any of the powers conferred onthe Monetary Authority by Part V or VI, exercise one or more of the following powers-

(i) to confirm, vary or reverse any requirement, appointment or direction made by the Monetary Authority;

(ii) (*Repealed*)

(iii) to direct the Financial Secretary to present a petition to the High Court for the winding-up of the authorized institution or former authorized institution by the High Court.

(2) The Governor in Council may, before considering any report or appeal under subsection (1), seek the advice of the Banking Advisory Committee or the Deposit-taking Companies Advisory Committee, or both, but shall not be bound to follow any such advice.

(3) (*Repealed*)

Notification of direction under section 52(1)(B) or (C), etc.

53A.(1) A direction given under section 52(1)(B) or (C) shall-

(a) be in writing;

(b) be served on the authorized institution specified in the direction at its principal place of business in Hong Kong;

(c) take effect immediately it is so served; and

(d) state the name and address of the Advisor or Manager, as the case may be, appointed in respect of that institution.

(2) A variation under section 52(3A) of a direction given under section 52(1)(C) shall-

(a) be in writing;

(b) be served on-

(i) the authorized institution specified in the direction at its principal place of business in Hong Kong except that, in the case of an authorized institution incorporated outside Hong Kong, it shall be served on the institution's principal place of business outside Hong Kong; and

        (ii)   the Manager of the institution; and

    (c)   take effect immediately it is so served, unless otherwise specified in the variation.

(3) A direction in writing given under section 52(1)(C), and a variation in writing under section 52(3A) of such a direction, include a copy of the direction or variation, as the case may be.

(4) Notice of a direction given under section 52(1)(C) shall be published by the Monetary Authority by notice in the Gazette and in such other ways as appear to him expedient for notifying the public.

(5) Subsection (4) shall apply to a notice under section 52(3G) as it applies to a direction given under section 52(1)(C).

Effect of direction under section 52(1)(C)

53B.(1)   Subject to subsection (2) and section 53C(3)(a)(i), (b) and (c), immediately upon a direction given under section 52(1)(C) coming into force-

    (a)   in respect of an authorized institution incorporated in Hong Kong, any appointment of a person as a chief executive or director of the institution which was in force immediately before that direction came into force;

    (b)   in respect of an authorized institution incorporated outside Hong Kong, any appointment of a person as a chief executive of the institution (in so far as such appointment relates to the business in Hong Kong of the institution) which was in force immediately before that direction came into force,

shall be deemed to be revoked and, accordingly, that person shall not act or continue to act as any such chief executive or director, as the case may be, during the period for which that direction is in force.

(2) An appointment referred to in subsection (1) shall not be revoked under that subsection where the direction concerned given under section 52(1)(C) expressly provides that the appointment shall not be so revoked.

(3) An authorized institution is not required to give any notice to the Monetary Authority pursuant to section 72A(2A) as a consequence of the operation of subsection (1).

(4) During the period for which a direction given under section 52(1)(C) is in force in respect of an authorized institution incorporated in Hong Kong-

(a) no meeting of the institution may be held except with the consent, and in the presence, of the Manager of the institution;

(b) no resolution may be passed at a meeting of the institution except with the consent of the Manager of the institution.

(5) Subject to section 53D, it is hereby declared that-

(a) any resolution passed, or purporting to have been passed, in contravention of subsection (4)(b);

(b) any thing done in reliance on any such resolution,

shall be invalid by reason of that contravention.

(6) Where-

(a) any member or director of an authorized institution requests the Manager of the institution to give a consent referred to in subsection (4)(a) in relation to the institution, the Manager shall not unreasonably refuse to give such consent;

(b) such consent is given, the Manager shall attend the meeting of the institution to which such consent relates.

(7) During the period for which a direction given under section 52(1)(C) is in force in respect of an authorized institution incorporated outside Hong Kong-

(a) the institution shall, in respect of any proposed resolution which, whether directly or indirectly, may affect any of the affairs, business and property of the institution, submit to the Manager of the institution, not later than 14 days before the meeting of the institution at which the resolution is to be moved (or such shorter period as is approved by the Manager in any particular case)-

(i) a copy of the resolution; and

(ii) notice in writing of the date, time and place of the meeting;

(b) the Manager may, in respect of a resolution referred to in paragraph (a), by notice in writing served on the institution at its principal place of business outside Hong Kong before the time specified in the notice under paragraph (a)(ii) as being the time

at which the meeting of the institution at which the resolution is to be moved is to be held, object to that resolution if, in his opinion, that resolution, if passed, might adversely affect or conflict with the discharge of his duties or the exercise of his powers in respect of any of the affairs, business and property of the institution.

(8) Subject to section 53D, it is hereby declared that-

(a) any resolution referred to in subsection (7)(a) passed or purporting to have been passed, and in respect of which the Manager of the authorized institution concerned-

(i) has not received a copy thereof under subsection (7)(a)(i);

(ii) has not received notice under subsection (7)(a)(ii) of the date, time and place of the meeting at which the resolution was moved; or

(iii) has made an objection under subsection (7)(b);

(b) any thing done in reliance on any such resolution,

shall be invalid-

(i) by reason of paragraph (a)(i), (ii) or (iii), as the case may be; and

(ii) to the extent that the resolution relates to any of the affairs, business and property of the institution,

until such time, if any, as the Manager, with the consent of the Monetary Authority,serves on the institution at its principal place of business outside Hong Kong a notice in writing stating that the resolution is approved with effect on and after the day on which such notice is so served.

(9) Any person who acts or continues to act as a chief executive or director of an authorized institution in contravention of subsection (1) commits an offence and is liable-

(a) on conviction upon indictment to a fine of $200,000 and to imprisonment for 2 years; or

(b) on summary conviction to a fine of $50,000 and to imprisonment for 6 months,

and, in the case of a continuing offence, to a further fine of $5,000 for every day during which the offence continues.

(10) In this section, "meeting", in relation to an authorized institution-

    (a)   means-

        (i)   any general meeting of the members of the institution; or

        (ii)   any meeting of the directors of the institution; and

    (b)   if the institution is incorporated outside Hong Kong, includes any meeting of the creditors of the institution.

Powers of Manager

53C.(1) Subject to the primary objective or objectives with which he shallcomply, the Manager of an authorized institution-

    (a)   may do all such things as may be necessary for the management of the affairs, business and property of the institution; and

    (b)   without limiting the generality of paragraph (a), shall have, and may exercise, in respect of that institution, all the powers specified in the Ninth Schedule.

(2) The Manager of an authorized institution may require any person who has ceased to be or who is still a chief executive or director of the institution by virtue of section 53B(1) or (2), as the case may be, to submit such information in relation to the affairs, business and property of the institution as the Manager may reasonably require for the discharge of his duties or the exercise of his powers in respect of the institution, and such information shall be submitted within such period and in such manner as the Manager may require.

(3) Subject to subsection (4), the Manager of an authorized institution

may-

    (a)   if the institution is incorporated in Hong Kong-

        (i)   appoint any person (including a person referred to in section 53B(1)(a)) to be a chief executive or director of the institution, whether to fill a vacancy arising from the operation of section 53B(1)(a) or otherwise;

(ii)   at any meeting of the members of the institution, move any resolution which is seconded by a member or which has the approval of the Monetary Authority;

(iii)   at any meeting of the directors of the institution, move any resolution which is seconded by a director or which has the approval of the Monetary Authority;

(iv)   call any meeting of the members, directors or creditors of the institution;

(b)   if the institution is incorporated outside Hong Kong, appoint any person (including a person referred to in section 53B(1)(b)) to be a chief executive in respect of the business in Hong Kong of the institution, whether to fill a vacancy arising from the operation of section 53B(1)(b) or otherwise;

(c)   revoke any appointment to which section 53B(2) applies or made pursuant to paragraph (a)(i) or (b).

(4) The Manager of an authorized institution shall not exercise any power conferred on him under subsection (3)(a)(i), (ii) or (iii), (b) or (c) except with the approval of the Monetary Authority.

(5) Section 71(1) shall not apply to any appointment made pursuant to subsection (3)(a)(i) or (b).

(6) An authorized institution is not required to give any notice to the Monetary Authority pursuant to section 72A(2A) as a consequence of any appointment, or the revocation of any appointment, made pursuant to subsection (3)(a)(i), (b) or (c).

(7) During the period for which a direction given under section 52(1)(C) is in force in respect of an authorized institution, any power conferred on-

(a)   the institution or a member, director, chief executive, manager or officer of the institution, whether by-

(i)   this Ordinance or the Companies Ordinance (Cap. 32);

(ii)   the memorandum or articles of association (including, in the case of an authorized institution incorporated outside Hong Kong, the equivalent, in the place where it is incorporated, of the memorandum or articles of association); or

(iii)   any other instrument under which it is incorporated;

> *(b)*   if the institution is incorporated outside Hong Kong, any relevant office-holder,

which could be exercised in such a way as to interfere with the exercise by the Manager of the institution of his powers is not exercisable except with the consent of the Manager, which consent may be given either generally or in any particular case.

(8) For the avoidance of doubt, it is hereby declared that during the period for which a direction given under section 52(1)(C) is in force in respect of an authorized institution incorporated outside Hong Kong, where there is any conflict or inconsistency between-

> *(a)*   a direction given by the Manager of the institution (including a direction to a person referred to in paragraph (b)); and

> *(b)*   a direction given by a member, director, chief executive, manager or officer of the institution or any relevant office-holder,

in relation to the affairs, business and property of the institution, the direction referred to in paragraph (a) shall, to the extent of the conflict or inconsistency, as the case may be, prevail over the direction referred to in paragraph (b).

(9) Subject to the primary objective or objectives with which he shall comply, in exercising his powers the Manager of an authorized institution shall be deemed to act as the institution's agent and, in relation thereto, section 9 of the Prevention of Bribery Ordinance (Cap. 201) shall apply to-

> *(a)*   the Manager acting as such agent; and

> *(b)*   any person who offers an advantage, within the meaning of that Ordinance, to the Manager acting as such agent, as if subsections (4) and (5) of that section were omitted.

(10)   A person dealing with the Manager of an authorized institution in good faith and for good consideration is not concerned to inquire whether the Manager is-

> *(a)*   acting within his powers;

> *(b)*   complying with the primary objective or objectives.

(11)   With the prior approval in writing of the Monetary Authority, the Manager of an authorized institution may, with or without restrictions as he thinks fit, delegate in writing to any person any of the duties and powers imposed or conferred on a Manager under this Ordinance except any such duty or power which he may not discharge or exercise, as the case may be, by virtue of a notice under section 52(3G).

(12) A delegate of the Manager of an authorized institution-

   (a)   shall discharge the delegated duties and may exercise the delegated powers as if the delegate were the Manager; and

   (b)   shall be presumed to be acting in accordance with the terms of the delegation in the absence of evidence to the contrary.

(13) Any person who fails without reasonable excuse to comply with any requirement under subsection (2) commits an offence and is liable-

   (a)   on conviction upon indictment to a fine of $200,000 and to imprisonment for 2 years and, in the case of a continuing offence, to a further fine of $10,000 for every day during which the offence continues; or

   (b)   on summary conviction to a fine of $50,000 and to imprisonment for 6 months and, in the case of a continuing offence, to a further fine of $5,000 for every day during which the offence continues.

(14) Any person who signs any document for the purposes of complying with any requirement under subsection (2) which he knows or reasonably ought to know to be false in a material particular commits an offense and is liable-

   (a)   on conviction upon indictment to a fine of $500,000 and to imprisonment for 2 years; or

   (b)   on summary conviction to a fine of $50,000 and to imprisonment for 6 months.

(15) Any person who produces any book, account, document, security or information for the purpose of complying with any requirement under subsection

(2) which is false in a material particular commits an offence and is liable-

   (a)   on conviction upon indictment to a fine of $500,000 and to imprisonment for 2 years; or

   (b)   on summary conviction to a fine of $50,000 and to imprisonment for 6 months.

(16) In this section, "relevant office-holder", in relation to an authorized institution incorporated outside Hong Kong, means any person acting-

> *(a)* in relation to the institution; and
>
> *(b)* in a place outside Hong Kong,

in any office similar to that of-

> **(i)** a liquidator, provisional liquidator, receiver or manager under the law of insolvency in Hong Kong;
>
> **(ii)** an administrator under the law of insolvency in the United Kingdom;
>
> **(iii)** an office specified in a notice under subsection (17) to be an office for the purposes of this definition.

(17) The Financial Secretary may, by notice in the Gazette, specify an office to be an office for the purposes of the definition of "relevant office-holder".

(18) It is hereby declared that a notice under subsection (17) is subsidiary legislation.

High Court may approve certain resolutions

53D.(1) During the period for which a direction given under section 52(1)(C) is in force in respect of an authorized institution incorporated in Hong Kong, the High Court may, on the application of-

> *(a)* the Manager of the institution; or
>
> *(b)* not less than 100 members of, or members holding not less than one-tenth of the total number of issued shares in, the institution,

approve or refuse to approve any resolution which-

> **(i)** where paragraph (a) is applicable, was proposed to be moved at a general meeting of the members of the institution but which was not so moved because a quorum for the meeting was not obtained;
>
> **(ii)** where paragraph (a) or (b) is applicable, has been properly moved at a general meeting of the members of the institution but which has not, for whatever reason, been passed.

(2) During the period for which a direction given under section 52(1)(C) is in force in respect of an authorized institution incorporated outside Hong Kong, the High Court may, on the application of the institution, approve or refuse to approve any resolution-

    (a)   which has been passed, or which purports to have been passed, at a meeting within the meaning of section 53B(10);

    (b)   which is invalid by reason of section 53B(8)(a)(iii); and

    (c)   a copy of which has been provided, in the form in which it was passed, or purports to have been passed, as the case may be, to the Manager by the institution not later than 14 days after the day on which it was passed, or purports to have been passed, as the case may be.

(3)   On the hearing of an application under subsection (1)

    (a)   the Manager and any member of the authorized institution concerned; and

    (b)   the Monetary Authority,

shall be entitled to be heard on the application and to call, examine and cross-examine any witness and, if he so thinks fit, support or oppose the making of the application.

(4)   On the hearing of an application under subsection (2)-

    (a)   the Manager, any chief executive (other than a chief executive who either holds his appointment by virtue of the operation of

            section 53B(2) or is appointed under section 53C(3)(b)) and a director of the authorized institution concerned, and any relevant office-holder within the meaning of section 53C(1 6); and

    (b)   the Monetary Authority,

shall be entitled to be heard on the application and to call, examine and cross-examine any witness and, if he so thinks fit, support or oppose the making of the application.

(5) Where the High Court approves a resolution referred to in subsection(1) or (2), then the resolution shall be deemed to have been passed upon, and shall take effect on and after, that approval or such later time as the High Court thinks fit.

(6) For the avoidance of doubt, it is hereby declared that where the High Court approves a resolution referred to in subsection (1) (where paragraph (ii) of that subsection is applicable) or (2), then section 53B(5) or (8), as the case may be, shall cease to apply to or in relation to the resolution on and after that approval takes effect.

High Court may make certain orders

53E.(1)   Where, on the application of the Manager of an authorized institution at any time during the period for which a direction given under section 52(1)(C) is in force in respect of the institution, it appears to the High Court that-

(a)   any person is about to do an act which, if done, might adversely affect or conflict with; or

(b)   any person has done an act which adversely affects or conflicts with,

the discharge of the Manager's duties or the exercise of the Manager's powers in respect of any of the affairs, business or property of the institution, then, subject to subsection (4), the High Court may, without prejudice to the operation of any of the other provisions of this Part or to any order the High Court would be entitled to make otherwise than by or by virtue of this section, make one or more of the following orders-

(i)   if paragraph (a) is applicable, an order restraining the person referred to in that paragraph from doing the act referred to in that paragraph;

(ii)   if paragraph (b) is applicable-

(A)   an order declaring the act referred to in that paragraph to be invalid with effect on and after the

date on which the order is made (but without prejudice to the validity of such act, or any thing done in reliance on such act, before that date);

(B)   an order declaring any thing done in reliance on such act to be invalid with effect on and after the date on which the order is made (but without prejudice to the validity of such act, or any thing done in reliance on such act, before that date);

(iii)   for the purpose of securing compliance with any other order under this section, an order directing a person to do or refrain from doing a specified act;

(iv)   any ancillary order which the High Court considers necessary in consequence of the making of any other order under this section.

(2) The High Court may, before making an order under subsection (1), direct that notice of the application under that subsection be given to such persons as it thinks fit or direct that notice of the application be published in such manner as it thinks fit, or both.

(3) Subject to subsection (4), the High Court may, of its own volition or on an application made to it for that purpose, by order reverse, vary or discharge an order made under subsection (1) or suspend the operation of such an order.

(4) The High Court shall, before making an order under subsection (1) or (3), satisfy itself, so far as it can reasonably do so, that the order would not unfairly prejudice any person.

Duration of direction under section 52(1)(B) or (C)

53F.(1) The Monetary Authority shall revoke a direction given under section 52(1)(B) or (C) if-

> *(a)* after consultation with the Financial Secretary, it appears to the Monetary Authority that it is no longer necessary for the direction to remain in force; or
>
> *(b)* it is necessary to do so to give effect to-
>
> > **(i)** a decision of the Governor in Council under section 53(1)(i); or
> >
> > **(ii)** an order of the Governor in Council under subsection (2).

(2) The Governor in Council, upon the application of-

> *(a)* in the case of an authorized institution the subject of a direction given under section 52(1)(B), the institution;
>
> *(b)* in the case of an authorized institution incorporated in Hong Kong the subject of a direction given under section 52(1)(C), not less than 100 members of, or members holding not less than one-tenth of the total number of issued shares in, the institution;
>
> *(c)* in the case of an authorized institution incorporated outside Hong Kong the subject of a direction given under section 52(1)(C), any chief executive (other than a chief executive who either holds his appointment by virtue of the operation of section 53B(2) or is appointed under section 53C(3)(b)) or director of the institution, or any relevant office-holder within the meaning of section 53C(16),

may, if he is satisfied that it is no longer necessary for the direction to remain in force, order the Monetary Authority to revoke that direction.

(3) The revocation under subsection (1) of a direction given under section 52(1)(B) or (C) shall-

      (a)   be in writing;

      (b)   be served on-

          (i)   the authorized institution specified in the direction at its principal place of business in Hong Kong except that, in the case of a direction given under section 52(1)(C) in respect of an authorized institution incorporated outside Hong Kong, it shall be served on the institution's principal place of business outside Hong Kong; and

          (ii)   the Advisor or Manager, as the case may be, of that institution; and

      (c)   take effect immediately it is so served unless otherwise specified in the revocation.

(4) Notice of a revocation under this section of a direction given under section 52(1)(C) shall be published by the Monetary Authority in the Gazette and in such other ways as appear to him expedient for notifying the public.

(5) A revocation in writing under subsection (1) of a direction given under section 52(1)(B) or (C) includes a copy of the revocation.

(6) For the avoidance of doubt, it is hereby declared that the revocation under subsection (1) of a direction given under section 52(1)(C) shall not revive any appointment deemed to be revoked as a consequence of the operation of section 53B(1).

Advisors, Managers and assistants

53G.(1) An Advisor or Manager may at any time by notice in writing to the Monetary Authority resign his office, but any such resignation shall not take effect unless and until it is accepted by the Monetary Authority.

(2) The Monetary Authority may at any time revoke the appointment of an Advisor or Manager.

(3) Where the office of an Advisor or Manager becomes vacant pursuant to subsection (1) or (2), or due to the death of the holder of that office, the Monetary Authority shall forthwith-

(a)   appoint a person to fill the vacancy; and

(b)   serve a notice in writing, specifying the name and address of the person so appointed, on the authorized institution concerned at its principal place of business in Hong Kong except that, in the case of an authorized institution incorporated outside Hong Kong the subject of a direction given under section 52(1)(C), it shall be served on the institution's principal place of business outside Hong Kong.

(**4**) The appointment of an Advisor or Manager shall be deemed to be revoked immediately upon the revocation under section 53F(1) of the direction given under section 52(1)(B) or (C) by virtue of which he holds his office.

(**5**) Subject to subsection (6), an Advisor or Manager may appoint such technical and professional persons (including any person who has been appointed under section 5A(3) of the Exchange Fund Ordinance (Cap. 66)) as he thinks fit to assist him in the discharge of his duties and exercise of his powers in respect of any of the affairs, business or property of the authorized institution concerned.

(**6**) An Advisor or Manager shall not exercise his power under subsection (5)-

(a)   unless he has the approval in writing of the Monetary Authority to do so; and

(b)   except in accordance with the conditions, if any, specified in the approval.

(**7**) The Monetary Authority, after consultation with the Financial Secretary, may at any time determine the remuneration and expenses to be paid by an authorized institution to-

(a)   the Advisor of the institution or any person appointed under subsection (5) by the Advisor;

(b)   the Manager of the institution or any person appointed under that subsection by the Manager,

and any such determination may be made whether or not-

(**i**)   the appointment of the Advisor or Manager or any such person has been revoked or has otherwise terminated;

(**ii**)   the direction concerned given under section 52(1)(B) or (C) has been revoked.

(**8**)   Where the Monetary Authority has made a determination under subsection

(7), he shall-

(a) if the determination relates to an Advisor of an authorized institution or to any person appointed under subsection (5) by the Advisor, serve a copy of the determination on the institution at its principal place of business in Hong Kong;

(b) if the determination relates to the Manager of an authorized institution or to any person appointed under subsection (5) by the Manager-

    (i) as soon as is reasonably practicable, publish a notice in the Gazette stating-

        (A) that the determination has been made; and

        (B) the name of that institution;

    (ii) if the institution is incorporated in Hong Kong, provide a copy of the determination to any member of the institution who so requests;

    (iii) if the institution is incorporated outside Hong Kong, serve a copy of the determination on the institution at its principal place of business outside Hong Kong and provide a copy of the determination to the chief executive (other than a chief executive who either holds his appointment by virtue of the operation of section 53B(2) or is appointed under section 53C(3)(b)), director or member of the institution, or any relevant office-holder within the meaning of section 53C(16), who so requests.

(9) Where a determination has been made under subsection (7), then any person aggrieved by the determination may appeal to the Governor in Council against the determination, but that determination shall take effect immediately, notwithstanding that an appeal has been or may be made under this subsection.

(10) Without prejudice to the generality of section 131, the Monetary Authority may, after consultation with the Financial Secretary, use the Exchange Fund established by the Exchange Fund Ordinance (Cap. 66) to pay, either in whole or in part, any remuneration and expenses payable pursuant to a determination under subsection (7).

Obstruction, etc. of Manager

53H. Any person who wilfully obstructs, resists or delays-

(a) the Manager of an authorized institution in the lawful discharge of his duties, or the lawful exercise of his powers, in respect of the institution; or

(b) any other person lawfully assisting the Manager in such discharge of such duties or such exercise of such powers,

commits an offence and is liable-

(i) on conviction upon indictment to a fine of $1,000,000 and to imprisonment for 5 years and, in the case of a continuing offence, to a further fine of $50,000 for every day during which the offence continues; or

(ii) on summary conviction to a fine of $50,000 and to imprisonment for 2 years and, in the case of a continuing offence, to a further fine of $5,000 for every day during which the offence continues.

54. *(Repealed)*

Examination and investigation of authorized institutions, etc.

55.(1) Without limiting the generality of section 52, the Monetary Authority may at any time, with or without prior notice to the authorized institution, examine the books, accounts and transactions of any authorized institution and, in the case of an authorized institution incorporated in Hong Kong, any local branch, overseas branch, overseas representative office or subsidiary, whether local or overseas, of such institution.

(2) Without limiting the generality of section 52, the Monetary Authority shall investigate the books, accounts and transactions of an authorized institution-

(a) if shareholders of the institution holding not less than one-third of the total number of issued shares in the institution, or depositors holding not less than one-tenth of the gross amount of the total deposit liabilities in Hong Kong of the institution or a sum equal to the aggregate of the paid-up share capital of the institution and its published reserve, whichever is the greater, apply to him to make such an investigation and submit to him such evidence as he considers necessary to justify the

investigation and furnish such security for the payment of the costs of the investigation as he may require; or

(b)   if the institution suspends payment or informs him of its intention to suspend payment.

(3) Where an investigation is made by the Monetary Authority pursuant to subsection (2), the Financial Secretary may order that all expenses incurred in such investigation shall be defrayed-

(a)   by the authorized institution; or

(b)   if the investigation was made pursuant to subsection (2)(a), either wholly by the persons who applied for the making of the investigation or partly by the authorized institution in such proportions as he considers to be just.

Production of authorized institution's books, etc.

56.(1) For the purposes of an examination or investigation under section 55, an authorized institution and, in the case of an authorized institution incorporated in Hong Kong, any local branch, overseas branch, overseas representative office or subsidiary, whether local or overseas, of such institution shall afford the person carrying out the examination or investigation access to its books and accounts, to documents of title to its assets and other documents, to all securities held by it in respect of its customers' transactions and its cash and to such information and facilities as may be required to conduct the examination or investigation, and shall produce to the person carrying out the examination or investigation such books, accounts, documents, securities, cash or other information as he may require:

Provided that, so far as is consistent with the conduct of the examination or investigation, such books, accounts, documents, securities and cash shall not be required to be produced at such times and such places as shall interfere with the proper conduct of the normal daily business of the institution, local branch, overseas branch, overseas representative office or subsidiary, as the case may be.

(2) Every director and every manager of an authorized institution which, without reasonable excuse, contravenes this section (which contravention shall include a contravention by any of the institution's local branches, overseas branches, overseas representative offices or subsidiaries) commits an offence and is liable-

(a)   on conviction upon indictment to a fine of $100,000 and to imprisonment for 12 months; or

(b)   on summary conviction to a fine of $50,000 and to imprisonment for 6 months,

and, in the case of a continuing offense, to a further fine of $5,000 for every day during which the offence continues.

(3) If any authorized institution or any local branch, overseas branch,overseas representative office or subsidiary of the institution produces any book,account, document, security or information whatsoever under this section whichis false in a material particular, every director and every manager of the institution commits an offence and is liable -

> *(a)*   on conviction upon indictment to a fine of $500,000 and to imprisonment for 2 years; or

> *(b)*   on summary conviction to a fine of $50,000 and to imprisonment for 6 months.

57-58. *(Repealed)*

PART XI - Audits And Meetings

Audit

59.(1) Every authorized institution, and its auditors, shall comply with theCompanies Ordinance (Cap. 32) with respect to the audit of a company's accounts, whether or not the institution is incorporated under that Ordinance.

(2) The Monetary Authority may, after consultation with an authorized institution, by notice in writing to the institution require the institution to submit to him a report-

> *(a)*   subject to subsection (3), prepared by an auditor or auditors appointed by the institution;

> *(b)*   on such matters as the Monetary Authority may reasonably require for the exercise of his functions under this Ordinance including, but without limiting the generality of such matters, such a report-

>> **(i)**   on the state of affairs or profit and loss, or both, of the institution based on an audit of the institution's accounts carried out in respect of the period specified in the notice requiring such a report; or

>> **(ii)**   on whether or not the institution has in place systems of control which are adequate to enable, as much as is practicable, the affairs, business and property of the institution to be prudently managed and the institution to comply with its duties under this Ordinance; and

> *(c)*   within such period and prepared in such manner as the Monetary Authority may reasonably require.

(3) The auditor or auditors appointed by an authorized institution to prepare a report required under subsection (2) shall be-

> *(a)*   an auditor or auditors appointed by the institution prior to the report being so required and approved by the Monetary Authority for the purpose of preparing the report;

> *(b)*   an auditor approved, or an auditor from amongst auditors nominated, by the Monetary Authority for the purpose of preparing the report after consultation with the institution; or

(c)   an auditor referred to in paragraph (a) and an auditor referred to
          in paragraph (b),

as may be required by the Monetary Authority.

(4) Section 60(1) shall not apply to anything done for the purposes of subsection (2)(b)(i) unless otherwise specified by the Monetary Authority by notice in writing to the authorized institution concerned.

(5) Every director and every manager of an authorized institution which contravenes subsection (1) or (2) commits an offence and is liable-

(a)   on conviction upon indictment to a fine of $200,000 and to
          imprisonment for 2 years and, in the case of a continuing
          offence under subsection (2), to a further fine of $10,000 for
          every day during which the offence continues; or

(b)   on summary conviction to a fine of $50,000 and to
          imprisonment for 6 months and, in the case of a continuing
          offence under subsection (2), to a further fine of $5,000 for
          every day during which the offence continues.

(6) In this section-

"adequate", in relation to systems of control, includes operating effectively;

"systems of control" includes procedures.

Notification in respect of auditors

59A.(1)   An authorized institution incorporated in Hong Kong shall immediately give written notice to the Monetary Authority if-

(a)   the institution-

(i)   proposes to give notice to its members of an ordinary
          resolution removing an auditor before the expiration of
          his term of office; or

(ii)   gives notice to its members of an ordinary resolution
          replacing an auditor at the expiration of his term of
          office; or

(b)   a person ceases to be an auditor of the institution otherwise than
          in consequence of such a resolution.

(2) An auditor of an authorized institution appointed under section 131 of the Companies Ordinance (Cap. 32) shall immediately give written notice to the Monetary Authority if he-

   (a)   resigns before the expiration of his term of office;

   (b)   does not seek to be re-appointed; or

   (c)   decides to include in his report on the institution's accounts any qualification or adverse statement as to a matter mentioned in section 141 of the Companies Ordinance (Cap. 32).

(3) Every director and every manager of an authorized institution which contravenes subsection (1) commits an offence and is liable-

   (a)   on conviction upon indictment to a fine of $200,000 and to imprisonment for 2 years and to a further fine of $10,000 for every day for which the institution fails to give the notice required under that subsection to the Monetary Authority; or

   (b)   on summary conviction to a fine of $50,000 and to imprisonment for 6 months and to a further fine of $5,000 for every day for which the institution fails to give the notice required under that subsection to the Monetary Authority.

Publication of audited balance sheet, etc.

60.(1) Every authorized institution incorporated in Hong Kong shall, not later than 4 months after the close of each financial year, or within such further period as the Monetary Authority approves in writing, publish, in accordance with Part I of the Tenth Schedule, a notice-

   (a)   relating to the institution's audited annual accounts for that year;

   (b)   complying with the requirements of Part 2 of that Schedule; and

   (c)   in the specified form, if any.

(2) An authorized institution shall-

   (a)   lodge with the Monetary Authority a copy of each notice it is required under subsection (1) to publish; and

   (b)   so lodge such copy not later than 7 days before the publication of the notice of which it is a copy.

(3) Where an authorized institution has complied with subsection (1) in respect of a financial year, it shall, as soon as is practicable thereafter exhibit-

(a)   a copy of its audited annual accounts for that year;

(b)   a copy of the report of the auditors made pursuant to section 141 of the Companies Ordinance (Cap. 32);

(c)   a copy of the report of the directors laid or to be laid before the company in general meeting in accordance with section 129D(1) of that Ordinance;

(d)   the full and correct names of all persons who are directors or managers for the time being of the institution; and

(e)   the names of all subsidiaries, for the time being, of the institution,

in a conspicuous position in the principal place of business of the institution in Hong Kong and in each local branch and, in the case of each of the documents, until the next time a document of the same kind is so exhibited in compliance with this subsection.

(4) A copy of each of the documents referred to in subsection (3) shall be lodged with the Monetary Authority by an authorized institution, prior to first exhibition thereof under that subsection, with a list of the names of all companies of which, for the time being, its directors are also directors.

(5) Every authorized institution incorporated outside Hong Kong shall, not later than 6 months after the close of each financial year, or within such further period as the Monetary Authority approves in writing, lodge with the Monetary Authority-

(a)   a copy of its audited annual balance sheet (including any notes thereon), and a copy of the profit and loss account for that year;

(b)   a copy of the report of the auditor, or any person exercising a similar function in accordance with the law of the place in which the institution is incorporated, upon that annual balance sheet (including any notes thereon) and profit and loss account; and

(c)   a copy of the report of the directors with respect to the profit or

loss of the institution for that year and the state of the institution's affairs as at the end thereof where the law of the place in which the institution is incorporated requires such a report.

(6) The Monetary Authority may by notice in writing exempt an authorized institution which has complied with subsection (5) from section 59(1) subject to such conditions as he may think proper to attach thereto.

(7) Where an authorized institution has complied with subsection (5) in respect of a financial year, it shall, unless otherwise permitted by the Monetary Authority, as soon as practicable thereafter exhibit a copy of each document lodged with the Monetary Authority under that subsection-

> *(a)* in a conspicuous position in the principal place of business of the institution in Hong Kong and in each local branch; and

> *(b)* in the case of any such document, until the next time a document of the same kind is so exhibited in compliance with this subsection.

(8) The Monetary Authority may require any authorized institution tosubmit such further information as he may think necessary for the proper understanding of any document it has under subsection (2), (4) or (5) lodged with the Monetary Authority; and such information shall be submitted within such period and in such manner as the Monetary Authority may require.

(9) Every director and every manager of an authorized institution which contravenes subsection (1), (2), (3), (4), (5) or (7) commits an offence and is liable-

> *(a)* on conviction upon indictment to a fine of $200,000; or

> *(b)* on summary conviction to a fine of $50,000,

and, in the case of a continuing offence, to a further fine of $5,000 for every day during which the offence continues.

(10) Every director and every manager of an authorized institution which fails without reasonable excuse to comply with any requirement under subsection (8) commits an offence and is liable on conviction upon indictment or on summary conviction to a fine of $50,000 and to imprisonment for 6 months and, in the case of a continuing offence, to a further fine of $2,500 for every day during which the offence continues.

(11) In this section and the Tenth Schedule, "audited annual accounts", in relation to an authorized institution-

> *(a)* means the institution's balance sheet and profit and loss
>
> account, together with any notes thereon, which are subject to a report by the institution's auditor pursuant to section 141 of the Companies Ordinance (Cap. 32); and

    (b)   includes the institution's cash flow statement, together with any notes thereon, if that auditor expresses an opinion on the institution's cash flow in that report.

Communication by auditor with Monetary Authority

61.(1) No duty which an auditor of an authorized institution may be subject to shall be regarded as contravened by reason of his communicating in good faith to the Monetary Authority, whether or not in response to a request made by the Monetary Authority, any information or opinion on a matter of which he becomes aware in his capacity as auditor and which is relevant to any function of the Monetary Authority under this Ordinance.

(2)   Subsection (1) applies to an auditor of a former authorized institution and a former auditor as it applies to an auditor of an authorized institution.

62.   *(Repealed)*

PART XII - Disclosure Of Information By Authorized Institutions

Returns and information to be submitted to the Monetary Authority

63.(1) Every authorized institution shall submit to the Monetary Authority-

>   *(a)*   not later than 14 days after the last day of each calendar month a return showing the assets and liabilities of its principal place of business in Hong Kong and all local branches thereof at the close of business on the last business day or last day of that month; and

>   *(b)*   not later than 14 days after the last day of each quarter ending on 31 March, 30 June, 30 September and 31 December respectively, or upon any other day which may be approved by the Monetary Authority, a return relating to its principal place of business in Hong Kong and all local branches thereof as at the close of business on the last business day or last day of the preceding quarter:

Provided that the Monetary Authority may by permission in writing allow the returns referred to in paragraphs (a) and (b) to be submitted at less frequent intervals.

(2) The Monetary Authority may require an authorized institution to submit (including periodically submit) such further information as he may reasonably require for the exercise of his functions under this Ordinance and such information shall be submitted within such period (or, where such information is required periodically, within such periods) and in such manner as the Monetary Authority may require.

(2A)   The Monetary Authority may require-

>   *(a)*   any holding company of an authorized institution;

>   *(b)*   any subsidiary of any such holding company; or

>   *(c)*   any subsidiary of an authorized institution,

to submit such information-

>   **(i)**   in any case, as he may reasonably require for the exercise of his functions under this Ordinance;

>   **(ii)**   in the case of paragraph (a) or (b), that the Monetary
>
>   Authority considers is necessary to be submitted in the

> interests of the depositors or potential depositors of the authorized institution concerned; and

> **(iii)** within such period and in such manner as the Monetary Authority may require.

(3) The Monetary Authority may require an authorized institution to submit to him, on or before such date as he may reasonably specify in the requirement, a report prepared by, subject to subsection (3B), an auditor or auditors appointed by the institution as to whether or not, in the opinion of the auditor or auditors, a return submitted to him pursuant to subsection (1), or information submitted to him pursuant to subsection (2), by the institution is correctly compiled, in all material respects, from the books and records of the institution and, if not so correctly compiled, the nature and extent of the incorrectness.

(3A) The Monetary Authority may require an authorized institution to submit to him, on or before such date as he may reasonably specify in the requirement and, subject to subsection (3C), in respect of the period specified in the requirement, a report prepared by, subject to subsection (3B), an auditor or auditors appointed by the institution as to all or any of the following-

> *(a)* whether or not, during that period, in the opinion of the auditor or auditors, the institution had in place systems of control which were adequate to enable, as much as is practicable-

> > **(i)** the institution's returns or information to be correctly compiled, in all material respects, from the books and records of the institution;

> > **(ii)** the institution to comply with its duties under Parts XII, XV, XVII and XVIII;

> > **(iii)** if the institution is incorporated in Hong Kong, the institution to maintain adequate provision for depreciation or diminution in the value of its assets (including provision for bad and doubtful debts), for liabilities which will or may fall to be discharged by it and for losses which will or may occur,

and, if the opinion is that those systems were not adequate, the nature and extent of any inadequacies;

> *(b)* subject to subsection (3D), whether or not, during that period-

> > **(i)** there appears to the auditor or auditors to be any material contravention by the institution of any of the duties referred to in paragraph (a)(ii), and, if it so appears, the nature of the contravention and the evidence therefor;

(ii)   if the institution is incorporated in Hong Kong, it appears to the auditor or auditors that the institution has failed to maintain the adequate provision referred to in paragraph (a)(iii), and, if it so appears, the reasons or evidence therefor;

(iii)   subject to subsection (3E), there was any matter which, in the opinion of the auditor or auditors, adversely affects the financial position of the institution to a material extent, and if there was, the nature of the matter and the reason why the auditor or auditors is or are of that opinion.

(3B)   The auditor or auditors appointed by an authorized institution to prepare a report required under subsection (3) or (3A) shall be-

(a)   an auditor or auditors appointed by the institution prior to the report being so required and approved by the Monetary Authority for the purpose of preparing the report;

(b)   an auditor approved, or an auditor from amongst auditors nominated, by the Monetary Authority for the purpose of preparing the report after consultation with the institution; or

(c)   an auditor referred to in paragraph (a) and an auditor referred to in paragraph (b),

as may be required by the Monetary Authority.

(3C)   No period specified in a requirement under subsection (3A) shall exceed 12 months unless the Monetary Authority is satisfied that a longer period is required in the interests of depositors of the authorized institution concerned or the public interest.

(3D)   No report shall be required under subsection (3A) as to a matter referred to in paragraph (b) of that subsection unless the report is also required as to a matter referred to in paragraph (a) of that subsection.

(3E)   In relation to any authorized institution incorporated outside Hong Kong, subsection (3A)(b)(iii) shall apply only to its principal place of business in Hong Kong and its local branches, and shall do so as if that principal place of business

and those branches were collectively a separate authorized institution.

(3F)   In this section-

"adequate", in relation to systems of control, includes operating effectively;

"systems of control" includes procedures.

(4) Notwithstanding section 120, the Monetary Authority may prepare and publish consolidated statements aggregating the figures in the returns furnished under subsection (1).

(5) Every director and every manager of an authorized institution which contravenes subsection (1), or fails to comply with any requirement under subsection (3) or (3A), commits an offence and is liable on conviction upon indictment or on summary conviction to a fine of $50,000 and, in the case of a continuing offence, to a further fine of $5,000 for every day during which the offence continues.

(6) Every director and every manager of an authorized institution which fails without reasonable excuse to comply with any requirement under subsection (2), and every director and every manager of a holding company of an authorized institution, subsidiary of such holding company or subsidiary of an authorized institution which fails without reasonable excuse to comply with any requirement under subsection (2A), commits an offense and is liable

> *(a)* on conviction upon indictment to a fine of $200,000 and to imprisonment for 2 years and, in the case of a continuing offence, to a further fine of $10,000 for every day during which the offence continues; or
>
> *(b)* on summary conviction to a fine of $50,000 and to imprisonment for 6 months and, in the case of a continuing offence, to a further fine of $5,000 for every day during which the offence continues.

(7) Any person who signs any document for the purposes of this section which he knows or reasonably ought to know to be false in a material particular commits an offence and is liable-

> *(a)* on conviction upon indictment to a fine of $500,000 and to imprisonment for 2 years; or
>
> *(b)* on summary conviction to a fine of $50,000 and to imprisonment for 6 months.

Information on shareholding, etc.

64.(1) Every authorized institution shall, if so required by the Monetary Authority, inform him of the name and address of, and the nature of the business carried on by, every company -

> *(a)* in which the institution holds the beneficial ownership, directly or indirectly, of an aggregate of 20 per cent or more of the share capital;

(b)   where any director or manager of that company is also a director or manager of the institution;

(c)   where the name of that company has common features with the name of the institution;

(d)   which, by whatever means, acts in concert with the institution to promote the institution's business; or

(e)   the controller of which is also the controller of the institution.

(2) The Monetary Authority may require any authorized institution which has submitted to him information pursuant to subsection (1) to submit to him such further information as he may reasonably require for the exercise of his functions under this Ordinance.

(3) Information that is required to be submitted under this section shall be submitted within such period and in such manner as the Monetary Authority may require.

(4) Every director and every manager of an authorized institution which fails without reasonable excuse to comply with any requirement under this section commits an offence and is liable-

(a)   on conviction upon indictment to a fine of $200,000 and to imprisonment for 2 years and, in the case of a continuing offence, to a further fine of $10,000 for every day during which the offence continues; or

(b)   on summary conviction to a fine of $50,000 and to imprisonment for 6 months and, in the case of a continuing offence, to a further fine of $5,000 for every day during which the offence continues.

(5) Any person who signs any document for the purposes of this section which he knows or reasonably ought to know to be false in a material particular commits an offence and is liable-

(a)   on conviction upon indictment to a fine of $500,000 and to imprisonment for 2 years; or

(b)   on summary conviction to a fine of $50,000 and to imprisonment for 6 months.

(6) If an authorized institution produces any book, account, document, security or information under this section which is false in a material particular, every director and every manager of the institution commits an offence and is liable-

(a)   on conviction upon indictment to a fine of $500,000 and to imprisonment for 2 years; or

(b)   on summary conviction to a fine of $50,000 and to imprisonment for 6 months.

Alteration in constitution

65.(1) An authorized institution, within 30 days after the making of any alteration to the memorandum of association, articles of association or other instrument under which it is incorporated, shall furnish to the Monetary Authority particulars of such alteration in writing, verified by a director of the institution.

(2) Every director and every manager of an authorized institution which contravenes this section commits an offence and is liable on conviction upon indictment or on summary conviction to a fine of $50,000 and, in the case of a continuing offence, to a further fine of $5,000 for every day during which the offence continues.

Authorized institution to notify Monetary Authority

when it ceases to take deposits

66.(1) An authorized institution which ceases to carry on the business of taking deposits or, as the case may be, banking business, shall forthwith notify the Monetary Authority in writing of that fact.

(2) Every director and every manager of an authorized institution which fails to comply with this section commits an offence and is liable on conviction upon indictment or on summary conviction to a fine of $10,000.

Duty to report inability to meet obligations

67.(1) If any authorized institution is likely to become unable to meet its obligations or if it is about to suspend payment it shall forthwith report all relevant facts, circumstances and information to the Monetary Authority.

(2) Every director and every manager of an authorized institution which fails without reasonable excuse to comply with subsection (1) commits an offence and is liable-

(a)   on conviction upon indictment to a fine of $200,000 and to imprisonment for 2 years and, in the case of a continuing

offence, to a further fine of $10,000 for every day during which the offence continues; or

(b) on summary conviction to a fine of $50,000 and to imprisonment for 6 months and, in the case of a continuing offence, to a further fine of $5,000 for every day during which the offence continues.

Examination by authorities outside Hong Kong

68. The appropriate recognized banking supervisory authority of a place outside Hong Kong may, with the approval of the Monetary Authority, examine-

(a) the books, accounts and transactions of the principal place of business in Hong Kong, or any local branch, of an authorized

institution which-

(i) is incorporated in that place or in respect of which the Monetary Authority is of the opinion that the authority has primary supervisory responsibility; or

(ii) is incorporated in or outside Hong Kong and is a subsidiary of a company which is incorporated in that place or in respect of which the Monetary Authority is of the opinion that the authority has primary supervisory responsibility;

(b) the documents of any local representative office of a bank which-

(i) is incorporated in that place or in respect of which the Monetary Authority is of the opinion that the authority has primary supervisory responsibility; or

(ii) is incorporated outside Hong Kong and is a subsidiary of a company which is incorporated in that place or in respect of which the Monetary Authority is of the opinion that the authority has primary supervisory responsibility.

PART XIII - Ownership And Management Of Authorized Institutions

Amalgamation, etc. requires approval

69.(1) An authorized institution incorporated in Hong Kong shall not, without the prior approval in writing of the Monetary Authority-

(a) make any arrangement or enter into any agreement for the sale or disposal of all or any part of-

(i) in the case of a bank, its banking business; and

(ii) in the case of a restricted licence bank or a deposit-taking company, its business of taking deposits; or

(b) *(Repealed)*

(2) An authorized institution incorporated in Hong Kong which-

(a) makes any arrangement or enters into any agreement for the sale or disposal of all or any part of its business, irrespective of whether the arrangement or agreement is pursuant to an approval under subsection (1)(a); or

(b) makes any reconstruction of its capital,

shall give notice in writing of the arrangement, agreement or reconstruction, as the case may be, to the Monetary Authority as soon as practicable after making that arrangement, entering into that agreement or making that reconstruction, and-

(i) the notice shall be signed by a director of the institution; and

(ii) the institution shall provide the Monetary Authority with such

information in respect of that arrangement, agreement or reconstruction as he may require.

(3) An authorized institution aggrieved by a decision of the Monetary Authority refusing his approval for the purposes of subsection (1) may appeal to the Governor in Council against the decision, but the decision shall take effect immediately, notwithstanding that an appeal has been or may be made under this subsection.

(4) Every director and every manager of an authorized institution which contravenes subsection (1) commits an offence and is liable

(a)   on conviction upon indictment to a fine of $200,000 and to imprisonment for 2 years; or

(b)   on summary conviction to a fine of $50,000 and to imprisonment for 6 months.

(5) Every director and every manager of an authorized institution which contravenes subsection (2) commits an offence and is liable on conviction upon indictment or on summary conviction to a fine of $50,000 and, in the case of a continuing offence, to a further fine of $5,000 for every day during which the offence continues.

(6) If an authorized institution produces any information whatsoever under this section which is false in a material particular, every director and every manager of the institution commits an offence and is liable-

(a)   on conviction upon indictment to a fine of $500,000 and to imprisonment for 2 years; or

(b)   on summary conviction to a fine of $50,000 and to imprisonment for 6 months.

Provisions applicable to persons proposing to become controllers

of authorized institutions incorporated in Hong Kong

70.(1) This section shall apply to a person becoming or being-

(a)   a majority shareholder controller; or

(b)   an indirect controller,

of an authorized institution incorporated in Hong Kong as it applies to a person becoming or being, as the case may be, a minority shareholder controller of an authorized institution incorporated in Hong Kong.

(2)   In this section-

"conditional notice of consent" means a notice of consent referred to in   paragraph (b) of the definition of "notice of consent";

"notice of consent" means a notice in writing specifying that-

(a)   there is no objection to the person specified in that notice becoming or being, as the case may be, a minority shareholder controller of the authorized institution specified in that notice; or

(b)   the conditions subject to which there is no objection to the person specified in that notice becoming or being, as the case may be, a minority shareholder controller of the authorized institution specified in that notice;

"notice of objection" means a notice in writing objecting to the person specified in that notice becoming or being, as the case may be, a minority shareholder controller of the authorized institution specified in that notice.

(3) Subject to subsection (4), no person shall become a minority shareholder controller of an authorized institution incorporated in Hong Kong unless-

(a)   he has served on the Monetary Authority a notice in writing stating that he proposes to become such a controller; and

(b) either-

(i)   subject to subsection (17), the Monetary Authority has, before the expiration of 3 months from the date of service of that notice, served on him a notice of consent; or

(ii)   that period has expired without the Monetary Authority having served on him a notice of objection.

(4)   A notice referred to in subsection (3)(a) served on the Monetary Authority by a person shall not be regarded as compliance with that subsection except as respects that person becoming a minority shareholder controller of the authorized institution to which the notice relates before the expiration of 12 months from-

(a)   where that person has been served with a notice of consent, on the date on which he was so served;

(b)   where the period referred to in subsection (3)(b) has expired and neither of the events specified in that section has occurred, on the expiration of that period;

(c)   where that person has been served with a notice of objection in respect of which an appeal under subsection (15) has been successful, on the date on which the appeal was successful.

(5) Where a person-

(a)   becomes a minority shareholder controller of an authorized institution in contravention of subsection (3);

    (b)   did not know that the acts or circumstances by virtue of which he became such a controller were such as to have that effect; and

    (c)   subsequently becomes aware of the fact that he has become such a controller,

he shall serve on the Monetary Authority, not later than 14 days after becoming aware of that fact, a notice in writing stating that he has become such a controller.

(6)   Subject to subsections (7), (8), (9) and (10), the Monetary Authority may serve-

    (a)   a notice of consent; or

    (b)   a notice of objection,

on a person.

(7) Without limiting the generality of conditions which the Monetary Authority may specify in a conditional notice of consent, he may specify in the notice such conditions as he may think proper to safeguard the interests of depositors and potential depositors of the authorized institution specified in the notice.

(8) The Monetary Authority shall not serve a notice of objection on a person where the Monetary Authority is satisfied-

    (a)   that the person is a fit and proper person to become or to be, as the case may be, a minority shareholder controller of the authorized institution specified in the notice;

    (b)   that the interests of depositors and potential depositors of that institution would not be or are not, as the case may be, in some other manner threatened by that person becoming or being, as the case may be, such a controller; and

    (c)   where that person-

        (i)   is not presently such a controller, that, having regard to

            that person's likely influence on that institution if he was to become such a controller-

            (A)   if the Monetary Authority is of the opinion that that institution is presently conducting its business prudently, the institution is likely to continue so conducting its business;

      (B) if the Monetary Authority is of any other opinion, that person is likely to undertake adequate remedial action;

   (ii) is presently such a controller, that, having regard to that person's influence on that institution as such a controller-

      (A) if the Monetary Authority is of the opinion that that institution was conducting its business prudently before that person became such a controller, the institution is presently, and is likely to continue, so conducting its business;

      (B) if the Monetary Authority is of any other opinion, that person is presently undertaking, or is likely to undertake, adequate remedial action.

(9) The Monetary Authority shall not serve a conditional notice of consent or notice of objection on a person who has become a minority shareholder controller of an authorized institution-

   (a) unless he has become such a controller in contravention of subsection (3);

   (b) subject to subsection (17), after the expiration of 3 months immediately following the Monetary Authority becoming aware of such contravention.

(10) The Monetary Authority shall, before serving a conditional notice of consent or notice of objection on a person, serve on that person a preliminary notice in writing-

   (a) stating that the Monetary Authority is considering the service on him of a conditional notice of consent or notice of objection, as the case may be;

   (b) where the Monetary Authority is considering the service on him of-

      (i) a conditional notice of consent, specifying the conditions which the Monetary Authority proposes to specify in the notice;

      (ii) a notice of objection, specifying which of the matters referred to in subsection (8) in respect of which the Monetary Authority is not satisfied; and

(c)   stating that he may, within 1 month from the date of service of the preliminary notice, make written representations to the Monetary Authority.

(11) Where representations are made in accordance with subsection (10)(c), the Monetary Authority shall take them into account in deciding whether to serve the conditional notice of consent or notice of objection, as the case may be, concerned.

(12) A conditional notice of consent served on a person-

(a)   may specify conditions which were not specified in the preliminary notice served under subsection (10) on that person where-

(i)   that person consents to those conditions; or

(ii)   a subsequent preliminary notice specifying those conditions has been served under that subsection on that person; and

(b)   shall give particulars of the right conferred by subsection (15).

(13) A notice of objection served on a person-

(a)   shall, subject to paragraph (b), specify which of the matters referred to in subsection (8) in respect of which the Monetary Authority is not satisfied;

(b)   shall not specify any such matters which were not specified in the preliminary notice served under subsection (10) on that person; and

(c)   shall give particulars of the right conferred by subsection (15).

(14) The Monetary Authority shall not be obliged to disclose to a person any

particulars of the matters referred to in subsection (8) on which he is considering the service on him or has served on him, as the case may be, a notice of objection.

(15) Any person aggrieved by a decision of the Monetary Authority to serve a conditional notice of consent or notice of objection on him may appeal to the Governor in Council against the decision, but that decision shall take effect immediately, notwithstanding that an appeal has been or may be made under this subsection.

(16) Where the Monetary Authority pursuant to section 72A requires a person who has given a notice in writing under subsection (3)(a) or (5) to submit information, the time between imposing that requirement and the receipt of the information shall be added to the period referred to in subsection (3)(b) or (9)(b), as the case may be.

(17) The period referred to in subsection (3)(b) or (9)(b) (together with any extension under subsection (16)) shall not expire, if it would otherwise do so, until 14 days after the expiration of the period within which representations can be made in accordance with subsection (10)(c).

(18) Subject to subsection (19), any person who contravenes subsection (3) commits an offence and is liable-

      (a)   on conviction upon indictment to a fine of $500,000 and to imprisonment for 5 years; or

      (b)   on summary conviction to a fine of $50,000 and to imprisonment for 6 months.

(19) Where a person is charged with an offence under subsection (18), it shall be a defence to prove that he did not know that the acts or circumstances by virtue of which he became a minority shareholder controller of the authorized institution concerned were such as to have that effect.

(20) Any person who contravenes subsection (5) commits an offence and is liable-

      (a)   on conviction upon indictment to a fine of $200,000 and to imprisonment for 2 years; or

      (b)   on summary conviction to a fine of $50,000 and to imprisonment for 6 months,

and, in the case of a continuing offence, to a further fine of $5,000 for every day during which the offence continues.

(21) Any person who contravenes any condition specified in a conditional notice of consent served on him commits an offence and is liable-

      (a)   on conviction upon indictment to a fine of $200,000 and to imprisonment for 2 years; or

      (b)   on summary conviction to a fine of $50,000 and to imprisonment for 6 months,

and, in the case of a continuing offence, to a further fine of $5,000 for every day during which the offence continues.

Objection to existing controllers

70A.(1)   This section shall apply to a person being-

        (a)   a majority shareholder controller; or

        (b)   an indirect controller,

of an authorized institution incorporated in Hong Kong as it applies to a person being a minority shareholder controller of an authorized institution incorporated in Hong Kong.

(2) In this section, unless the context otherwise requires, "notice of objection" means a notice in writing objecting to the person specified in that notice being a minority shareholder controller of the authorized institution specified in that notice.

(3) Subject to subsection (4), the Monetary Authority may serve a notice of objection on a person-

        (a)   who is a minority shareholder controller of an authorized institution incorporated in Hong Kong where-

                (i)   his being such a controller is not in contravention of section 70(3); or

                (ii)   his being such a controller is in contravention of that section but the Monetary Authority is prohibited by virtue of section 70(9)(b) from serving a notice of objection under section 70(6) on him; and

        (b)   where it appears to the Monetary Authority that-

                (i)   that person is not or is no longer a fit and proper person to be such a controller;

                (ii)   the interests of depositors or potential depositors of that

                            institution may be in some other manner threatened by that person being such a controller; or

                (iii)   that person has contravened any condition specified in a conditional notice of consent served under section 70(6) on him.

(4)   The Monetary Authority shall, before serving a notice of objection on a person, serve on that person a preliminary notice in writing-

    (a)   stating that the Monetary Authority is considering the service on him of a notice of objection;

    (b)   specifying which of the matters referred to in subsection (3)(b) in respect of which the Monetary Authority is considering the service on him of the notice of objection; and

    (c)   stating that he may, within 1 month from the date of service of the preliminary notice, make written representations to the Monetary Authority.

(5) Where representations are made in accordance with subsection (4)(c), the Monetary Authority shall take them into account in deciding whether to serve the notice of objection concerned.

(6) A notice of objection-

    (a)   shall, subject to paragraph (b), specify which of the matters referred to in subsection (3)(b) on which the notice is served;

    (b)   shall not specify any such matters which were not specified in the preliminary notice served under subsection (4) on him; and

    (c)   shall give particulars of the right conferred by subsection (8).

(7) The Monetary Authority shall not be obliged to disclose to a person any particulars of the matters referred to in subsection (3)(b) on which he is considering the service on him or has served on him, as the case may be, a notice of objection.

(8) Any person aggrieved by a decision of the Monetary Authority to serve a notice of objection on him may appeal to the Governor in Council against the decision, but that decision shall take effect immediately, notwithstanding that an appeal has been or may be made under this subsection.

Restrictions on and sale of shares

70B.(1) This section shall apply to a person being a majority shareholder controller of an authorized institution incorporated in Hong Kong as it applies to a person being a minority shareholder controller of an authorized institution incorporated in Hong Kong.

(2) The powers conferred by this section shall be exercisable where a person-

    (a)   has become a minority shareholder controller of an authorized institution in contravention of section 70(3) in that-

        (i)   a notice in writing has been served under section 70(3)(a) on the Monetary Authority by that person in respect of

that institution but neither of the events specified in section 70(3)(b) has occurred;

    (ii)   no notice in writing has been served under section 70(5) in respect of that contravention;

    (iii)   a notice in writing has been served under section 70(5) on the Monetary Authority by that person in respect of that contravention, the Monetary Authority has served a notice of objection under section 70(6) on that person in respect of that contravention, and either-

        (A)   the period specified in the Administrative Appeals Rules (Cap. 1 sub. leg.) within which that person may appeal under section 70(15) against the decision of the Monetary Authority to serve such notice of objection has expired without any such appeal having been made; or

        (B)   an appeal under section 70(15) by that person against the decision of the Monetary Authority to so serve such notice of objection is unsuccessful; or

    (iv)   that person has been convicted of an offence under section 70(18) in respect of that contravention; or

    (b)   continues to be a minority shareholder controller of an authorized institution after having been served with a notice of objection under section 70A(3) in respect of his being such a controller and either-

        (i)   the period specified in the Administrative Appeals Rules (Cap. 1 sub. leg.) within which that person may appeal under section 70A(8) against the decision of the Monetary Authority to so serve such notice of objection has expired without any such appeal having been made; or

        (ii)   an appeal under section 70A(8) by that person against the decision of the Monetary Authority to so serve such notice of objection is unsuccessful.

(3)   Subject to subsection (8), the Monetary Authority may, by notice in writing served on the person concerned, direct that any specified shares to which this section applies shall, until further notice, be subject to one or more of the followingrestrictions-

(a) any transfer of those shares or, in the case of unissued shares, any transfer of the right to be issued with them, and any issue of such shares, shall be void;

(b) no voting rights shall be exercisable in respect of the shares;

(c) no further shares shall be issued in right of them or pursuant to any offer made to their holder;

(d) except in a liquidation, no payment shall be made of any sums due from the authorized institution, or other company, concerned on the shares, whether in respect of capital or otherwise.

(4) Where shares are subject to the restrictions under subsection (3)(a), any agreement to transfer the shares or, in the case of unissued shares, the right to be issued with them, shall be void.

(5) Where shares are subject to the restrictions under subsection (3)(c) or (d), an agreement to transfer any right to be issued with other shares in right of those shares, or to receive any payment on them (otherwise than in a liquidation), shall be void.

(6) Where shares are subject to any restrictions under subsection (3), any person affected by any of those restrictions may request the Monetary Authority to make an application referred to in subsection (7)(a) in respect of those shares and, where such a request is made, the Monetary Authority shall, not later than 1 month after that request has been made-

(a) if, by virtue of subsection (9), the Monetary Authority is prohibited from making such an application, serve a notice in writing on that person stating that he is so prohibited;

(b) in any other case-

(i) comply with that request; or

(ii) serve a notice in writing on that person stating that he does not propose to comply with that request.

(7) Subject to subsection (9), the High Court may-

(a) on the application of the Monetary Authority, order the sale of any specified shares to which this section applies and, if they are for the time being subject to any restrictions under subsection (3), that they shall cease to be subject to those restrictions;

(b) on the application of a person who has made a request under subsection (6) where-

(i) paragraph (b) of that subsection applies in respect of that request; and

(ii) he has been served with a notice in writing under paragraph (b)(ii) of that subsection in respect of that request; or

(iii) the period specified in that subsection has expired and neither of the events referred to in paragraph (b) of that subsection has occurred in respect of that request,

order the sale of any shares to which that request relates and that they shall cease to be subject to any restrictions under subsection (3).

(8) Where the Monetary Authority has, by virtue of subsection (2)(a)(ii), served a notice in writing under subsection (3) on the person concerned and-

(a) that person has, not later than 14 days after the service of that notice, served a notice in writing under section 70(5) on the Monetary Authority in respect of the contravention of section 70(3) to which that first-mentioned notice relates; and

(b) either-

(i) no notice of objection under section 70(6) has been served by the Monetary Authority on that person in respect of that contravention within the period in respect of which section 70(9)(b) permits such a notice of objection to be so served; or

(ii) such a notice of objection has been so served within that period but an appeal under section 70(15) by that person against the decision of the Monetary Authority to so serve such notice of objection is successful, whichever first occurs,

the Monetary Authority shall forthwith serve a notice in writing on that person to the effect that the first-mentioned notice is revoked.

(9) The Monetary Authority shall not, by virtue of subsection (2)(a)(ii), make an application referred to in subsection (7)(a) unless-

    (a) the application relates to shares which are the subject of a notice in writing under subsection (3); and

    (b) the person upon whom that notice has been served has not, within 14 days after the service of that notice, served a notice in writing under section 70(5) in respect of the contravention of section 70(3) to which that first-mentioned notice relates:

Provided that this subsection shall be without prejudice to the Monetary Authority's power, by virtue of subsection (2)(a)(iii), to subsequently make such an application in respect of those shares.

(10) Where an order has been made under subsection (7), the High Court may, on the application of the Monetary Authority, make such further order relating to the sale or transfer of the shares as it thinks fit.

(11) Where shares are sold pursuant to an order under this section, the proceeds of the sale, less the costs of the sale, shall be paid into court for the benefit of the persons beneficially interested in them, and any such person may apply to the High Court for an order that the whole or part of the proceeds be paid to him.

(12) This section shall apply

    (a) to all the shares in the authorized institution concerned by virtue of which the person concerned is a minority shareholder

        controller of the institution which are held by him or any associate of his and were not so held immediately before he became such a controller; and

    (b) where the person concerned became a minority shareholder controller of the authorized institution concerned by virtue of the acquisition by him or any associate of his of shares in another company, to all the shares in that company which are held by him or any associate of his and were not so held immediately before he became such a controller.

(13) A copy of a notice in writing served under subsection (3) or (8) on the person concerned shall be served on the authorized institution or other company to whose shares it relates and, if it relates to shares held by any associate of that person, on that associate.

(14) The Chief Justice may make rules regulating the practice and procedure in connection with applications (including any class of applications) made under subsection (7).

Prohibition on certain persons acting as indirect controllers

70C.(1) In this section, "prohibited person", in relation to an authorized institution, means any person-

(a)   who has been served with a notice of objection under section 70(6) in respect of his becoming or being, as the case may be, an indirect controller of the institution and either-

   (i)   the period specified in the Administrative Appeals Rules (Cap. I sub. leg.) within which that person may appeal under section 70(15) against the decision of the Monetary Authority to so serve such notice of objection has expired without any such appeal having been made; or

   (ii)   an appeal under section 70(15) by that person against the decision of the Monetary Authority to so serve such notice of objection is unsuccessful; or

(b)   who has been served with a notice of objection under section 70A(3) in respect of his being an indirect controller of the institution and either-

   (i)   the period specified in the Administrative Appeals Rules

   (Cap. 1 sub. leg.) within which that person may appeal under section 70A(8) against the decision of the Monetary Authority to so serve such notice of objection has expired without any such appeal having been made; or

   (ii)   an appeal under section 70A(8) by that person against the decision of the Monetary Authority to so serve such notice of objection is unsuccessful.

(2) No person who is a prohibited person in respect of an authorized institution shall act or continue to act, as the case may be, as an indirect controller of the institution and, accordingly, as such a controller shall not give or shall cease to give, as the case may be, any directions or instructions to the directors of the institution or of another company of which it is a subsidiary.

(3) Where any director of an authorized institution or of another company of which it is a subsidiary is given (whether directly or indirectly) any directions or instructions-

(a)   by a person whom the director knows, or ought reasonably to know, is a prohibited person in respect of the institution; and

(b)   which are, or might reasonably be construed as being, prohibited from being so given by virtue of subsection (2),

the director shall forthwith notify the Monetary Authority of those directions or instructions and the circumstances in which they were so given.

(4) Any prohibited person who contravenes subsection (2) commits an offence and is liable-

(a)   on conviction upon indictment to a fine of $500,000 and to imprisonment for 5 years; or

(b)   on summary conviction to a fine of $50,000 and to imprisonment for 6 months,

and, in the case of a continuing offence, to a further fine of $5,000 for every day during which the offence continues.

(5) Any director who without reasonable excuse contravenes subsection (3) commits an offence and is liable-

(a)   on conviction upon indictment to a fine of $200,000 and to imprisonment for 2 years; or

(b)   on summary conviction to a fine of $50,000 and to imprisonment for 6 months,

and, in the case of a continuing offence, to a further fine of $5,000 for every day during which the offence continues.

Punishment for attempted evasion of restrictions

70D.(1) Any person who-

(a)   exercises or purports to exercise any right to dispose of any shares which, to his knowledge, are for the time being subject to any restrictions under section 70B(3) or of any right to be issued with any such shares;

(b)   votes in respect of any such shares (whether as holder or proxy), or appoints a proxy to vote in respect of them;

(c) being the holder of any such shares, fails to notify of their being subject to those restrictions any person whom he does not know to be aware of that fact but does know to be entitled (apart from the restrictions) to vote in respect of those shares whether as holder or as proxy; or

(d) being the holder of any such shares, or being entitled to any right to be issued with other shares in right of them, or to receive any payment on them (otherwise than in a liquidation), enters into any agreement which is void under section 70B(4) or (5),

commits an offence and is liable-

(i) on conviction upon indictment to a fine of $200,000 and to imprisonment for 2 years; or

(ii) on summary conviction to a fine of $50,000 and to imprisonment for 6 months.

(2) Where shares in an authorized institution or another company are issued in contravention of restrictions under section 70B(3), or payments are made by an authorized institution or another company in contravention of such restrictions, every director and every manager of the authorized institution or other company, as the case may be, who knowingly and wilfully permits such an issue of shares or the making of such a payment, as the case may be, commits an offence and is liable-

(a) on conviction upon indictment to a fine of $200,000 and to imprisonment for 2 years; or

(b) on summary conviction to a fine of $50,000 and to imprisonment for 6 months.

Chief executives and directors require Monetary Authority's approval

71.(1) Subject to section 53C(5), no person shall -

(a) become the chief executive of an authorized institution, or a director of an authorized institution incorporated in Hong Kong, without the consent in writing of the Monetary Authority; or

(b) if he becomes such chief executive or director without such consent, act or continue to act as such chief executive or director, as the case may be, without such consent,

and for the purposes of this subsection consent may be given subject to such conditions as the Monetary Authority may think proper to attach thereto and shall be conveyed to the person, and the institution, concerned as soon as practicable.

(2)　Where the Monetary Authority refuses to give consent under subsection (1), he shall notify the person concerned in writing of his refusal as soon as practicable.

(3)　The Monetary Authority may by notice in writing to the person and the authorized institution concerned withdraw any consent given under subsection (1), or amend any condition attached to any such consent, if the Monetary Authority-

> *(a)*　has given to the chief executive or director concerned not less than 7 days' advance notice of his intention to do so, specifying his reasons; and

> *(b)*　has taken into account before so doing any written representation received by him from the chief executive or director concerned,

and in any such case the chief executive or director concerned shall cease to act as such or, as the case may be, shall comply with the amended conditions.

(4)　A person aggrieved-

> *(a)*　by a refusal to grant consent, or by conditions attached to a consent, under subsection (1);

> *(b)*　by the withdrawal of consent under subsection (3); or

> *(c)*　by the amendment under subsection (3) of conditions attached to a consent,

may appeal to the Governor in Council against the refusal, conditions, withdrawal or amendment, as the case may be, but such refusal, conditions, withdrawal or amendment shall take effect immediately notwithstanding that an appeal has been or may be made under this subsection.

(5)　Any person who contravenes subsection (1) or (3) commits an offence and is liable-

> *(a)*　on conviction upon indictment to a fine of $200,000 and to imprisonment for 2 years; or

> *(b)*　on summary conviction to a fine of $50,000 and to imprisonment for 6 months,

and, in the case of a continuing offence, to a further fine of $5,000 for every day during which the offence continues.

(6)   *(a)*   A person shall not be regarded for the purposes of subsection (1) as becoming a director of an authorized institution if he is appointed to serve as a director of it immediately on the expiration of a previous term by him as a director.

         (b)   A person who is a director of an authorized institution immediately prior to the commencement of this Ordinance shall for the purposes of this section be regarded as having the consent of the Monetary Authority under subsection (1) to continue to act as director.

         (c)   A person who is the chief executive of an authorized institution immediately prior to the commencement of the Banking (Amendment) Ordinance 1987 shall for the purposes of this section be regarded as having the consent of the Monetary Authority under subsection (1) to continue to act as chief executive.

(7) For the purposes of this section, where a person has the consent of the Monetary Authority under subsection (1) or by virtue of subsection (6)(c) to be or continue to act as the chief executive of an authorized institution, and is such chief executive, he is not required to have the consent of the Monetary Authority under subsection (1) to be or continue to act as a director of that institution.

72. *(Repealed)*

Monetary Authority may require specified persons to submit information

72A.(1) For the purposes of this section, "specified person" means-

     (a)   any person who proposes to become a controller of an authorized institution incorporated in Hong Kong;

     (b)   any person who is the chief executive of an authorized institution;

     (c)   any person who is a director or controller of an authorized institution incorporated in Hong Kong; or

     (d)   any person who is seeking the consent of the Monetary Authority under section 71(1).

(2) The Monetary Authority may require a specified person to submitsuch information as he may reasonably require for the exercise of his functions under this Ordinance and such information shall be submitted within such period and in such manner as the Monetary Authority may require.

(2A) Subject to section 53B(3), where an authorized institution becomes aware of the fact that any person has become or has ceased to be a specified person in respect of the institution, the institution shall, not later than 14 days after becoming aware of that fact, give notice in writing to the Monetary Authority of that fact.

(3) Any specified person (other than a person referred to in subsection (1)(a) or (d)) who fails without reasonable excuse to comply with any requirement under subsection (2) commits an offense and is liable

> *(a)*   on conviction upon indictment to fine of $200,000 and to imprisonment for 2 years and, in the case of a continuing offence, to a further fine of $10,000 for every day during which the offence continues; or

> *(b)*   on summary conviction to a fine of $50,000 and to imprisonment for 6 months and, in the case of a continuing offence, to a further fine of $5,000 for every day during which the offence continues.

(4) Any specified person who signs any document for the purposes of complying with any requirement under subsection (2) which he knows or reasonably ought to know to be false in a material particular commits an offence and is liable-

> *(a)*   on conviction upon indictment to a fine of $500,000 and to imprisonment for 2 years; or

> *(b)*   on summary conviction to a fine of $50,000 and to imprisonment for 6 months.

(5) Any specified person who produces any book, account, document, security or information for the purpose of complying with any requirement under subsection (2) which is false in a material particular commits an offence and is liable-

> *(a)*   on conviction upon indictment to a fine of $500,000 and to imprisonment for 2 years; or

> *(b)*   on summary conviction to a fine of $50,000 and to imprisonment for 6 months.

(6) Every director and every manager of an authorized institution which contravenes subsection (2A) commits an offence and is liable-

    (a)   on conviction upon indictment to a fine of $200,000 and to imprisonment for 2 years; or

    (b)   on summary conviction to a fine of $50,000 and to imprisonment for 6 months,

and, in the case of a continuing offence, to a further fine of $5,000 for every day during which the offence continues.

Certain persons prohibited from acting as employees of authorized institutions except with consent of Monetary Authority

73.(1) No person who-

    (a)   is bankrupt or has entered into a composition with his creditors;

    (b)   has been convicted in any place of an offence involving fraud or dishonesty; or

    (c)   knows, or ought reasonably to know, that, in respect of an authorized institution of which he is or was a director or is or was concerned in the management thereof-

        (i)   the institution is being, or has been, wound up or otherwise dissolved; or

        (ii)   its licence or registration, as the case may be, has been revoked,

shall, without the consent in writing of the Monetary Authority, become an employee of an authorized institution (or, where paragraph (c) is applicable, of another authorized institution) or, if becoming such an employee without such consent, act, or continue to act, as such employee.

(1A) No person who on or after becoming an employee of an authorized institution (and whether or not he became such an employee before, on or after the relevant day)-

    (a)   becomes bankrupt, or enters into a composition with his creditors, on or after the relevant day;

    (b)   is convicted, on or after the relevant day, in any place of an offence involving fraud or dishonesty; or

    (c)   knows, or ought reasonably to know, that, in respect of another authorized institution of which he is or was a director or is or was concerned in the management thereof-

(i)   the institution is being, or has been, wound up or otherwise dissolved on or after the relevant day; or

(ii)   its licence or registration, as the case may be, has been revoked on or after the relevant day,

shall-

(i)   in the case of paragraph (a) or (b), continue to act as such employee without the consent in writing of the Monetary Authority;

(ii)   in the case of paragraph (c), continue to act as such employee either-

(A)   unless he has notified the Monetary Authority of that prior employment together with a request that the Monetary Authority grant consent to him to continue to act as such employee; or

(B)   if the Monetary Authority refuses to grant such consent.

(1B)   Where the Monetary Authority refuses to grant consent under subsection (1) or (1A) he shall notify the person concerned in writing of his refusal as soon as practicable.

(1C)   A person aggrieved by a refusal to grant consent under subsection (1) or (1A) may appeal to the Governor in Council against the refusal, but such refusal shall take effect immediately notwithstanding that an appeal has been or may be made under this subsection.

(2)   Any person who contravenes subsection (1) or (1A) commits an offense and is liable-

    (a)   on conviction upon indictment to a fine of $100,000 and to imprisonment for 12 months; or

    (b)   on summary conviction to a fine of $50,000 and to imprisonment for 6 months.

(3)   In this section, "relevant day" means the day of commencement of the Banking (Amendment) Ordinance 1993 (94 of 1993).

Appointment of chief executive

74.(1)   Subject to sections 53B(1) and 53C(3), every authorized institution shall appoint a chief executive, and not less than one alternate chief executive, of the institution, each of whom shall be-

(a)   an individual; and

(b)   ordinarily resident in Hong Kong,

except that, in the case of an authorized institution incorporated outside Hong Kong, such chief executive and alternate chief executive are only required to be the chief executive or alternate chief executive, as the case may be, in respect of the business in Hong Kong of the institution.

(1A)   Where the chief executive of an authorized institution is precluded by illness, absence from Hong Kong or any other cause from carrying out his functions as the chief executive, an alternate chief executive of the institution shall act as such chief executive.

(2) Every director and every manager of an authorized institution which contravenes subsection (1) commits an offence and is liable on conviction upon indictment or on summary conviction to a fine of $50,000 and, in the case of a continuing offence, to a further fine of $5,000 for every day during which the offense continues.

PART XIV

75-78. *(Repealed)*

PART XV - Limitations On Loans By And Interests Of Authorized Institutions

Interpretation and application

79.(1) In this Part-

"non-listed company" means a company not listed on the Unified Exchange:

> Provided that any public statutory corporation designated for the purposes of this definition by the Financial Secretary by notice in the Gazette shall be deemed not to be a non-listed company;

relative" means-

> *(a)* any immediate ascendant, any spouse or former spouse of any such ascendant, and any brother or sister of any such spouse or former spouse;
>
> *(b)* any immediate descendant, and any spouse or former spouse of any such descendant;
>
> *(c)* any brother or sister, aunt or uncle and any nephew or niece and any first cousin;
>
> *(d)* any spouse or former spouse, any immediate ascendant of any such spouse or former spouse, and any brother or sister of any such spouse or former spouse,

and, for the purposes of this definition, any step-child shall be deemed to be the child of both its natural parent and of its step-parent and any adopted child to be the child of the adopting parent, and a spouse shall include anyone living as such;

"value" means-

(a)   in the case of shares in a company, the total of the current book value and the amount for the time being remaining unpaid on the shares; and

(b)   in any other case, the current book value.

(2) For the purposes of this Part, the capital base of an authorizedinstitution means the capital base of the institution as determined in accordance with the Third Schedule except that, for those purposes, any requirement under section 98(2) referred to in that Schedule shall not apply in determining such capital base.

(3) For the purposes of sections 83 and 85, "unsecured" means granted without security, or, in respect of any advance, loan or credit facility granted or financial guarantee or other liability incurred with security, any part thereof which at any time exceeds the market value of assets constituting that security; and "security" means such security as would, in the opinion of the Monetary Authority, be acceptable to a prudent banker.

(4) In relation to any authorized institution incorporated outside Hong Kong, sections 80, 82, 85, 86 and, to the extent that it relates to such an institution, section 91 shall apply only to its principal place of business in Hong Kong and its local branches, and shall do so as if that principal place ofbusiness and those branches were collectively a separate authorized institution.

(5) The Financial Secretary may, by notice in the Gazette, amend the definition of "relative".

Monetary Authority may require provisions of this Part to apply to certain

authorized institutions on a consolidated basis

79A.(1)   Subject to subsection (2), for the purposes of the application of any provision of this Part to an authorized institution incorporated in Hong Kong which has any subsidiary, the Monetary Authority may, by notice in writing to the institution, require the provision to apply to the institution-

(a)   on a consolidated basis instead of on an unconsolidated basis; or

(b)   on both a consolidated basis and an unconsolidated basis.

(2) The Monetary Authority may, in a notice under subsection (1) to an authorized institution, require the provision of this Part to which the notice relates to apply to the institution on a consolidated basis only in respect of such subsidiaries of the institution as are specified in the notice.

(3) No duty which a subsidiary of an authorized institution may be subject to shall be regarded as contravened by reason of the submission of information by the subsidiary to the institution for the purpose of enabling or assisting the institution to comply with a notice under subsection (1) to the institution.

Advance against security of own shares, etc.

80.(1) An authorized institution shall not grant any advances, loans or credit facilities (including letters of credit), or give any financial guarantee or incur any other liability, against the security of its own shares.

(2) An authorized institution shall not, except with the approval in writing of the Monetary Authority, which approval shall be subject to such conditions as the Monetary Authority may think proper to attach thereto, grant any advances, loans or credit facilities (including letters of credit), or give any financial guarantee or incur any other liability, against the security of the shares of-

  (a)   any holding company of the institution;

  (b)   any subsidiary of the institution; or

  (c)   any other subsidiary of any holding company of the institution.

(3) Every director and every manager of an authorized institution which contravenes subsection (1) or (2) commits an offence and is liable-

  (a)   on conviction upon indictment to a fine of $100,000 and to imprisonment for 12 months; or

  (b)   on summary conviction to a fine of $50,000 and to imprisonment for 6 months.

Limitations on advances by authorized institutions

81.(1) Subject to subsections (4), (4A), (5) and (6), the financial exposure of an authorized institution incorporated in Hong Kong to-

  (a)   any one person;

  (b)   two or more companies which-

    (i)   are subsidiaries of the same holding company; or

    (ii)   have the same controller (not being a company);

  (c)   any holding company and one or more of its subsidiaries; or

  (d)   any one person (not being a company) and one or more companies of which that person is a controller,

shall not exceed an amount equivalent to 25% of the capital base of the institution.

(2) The financial exposure of an authorized institution to any person, company or combination thereof referred to in subsection (1)(a), (b), (c) or (d) shall, for the purposes of this section, be taken to be the aggregate of-

> *(a)*   all advances, loans and credit facilities (including letters of credit) given to;

> *(b)*   the value of the institution's holdings of shares and debentures (within the meaning of those terms in section 2 of the Companies Ordinance (Cap. 32)) and other debt securities issued by; and

> *(c)*   the principal amount, multiplied by the factor specified by the Monetary Authority pursuant to subsection (3) for items referred to in Table B of the Third Schedule in relation to the institution where, in respect of that institution, the other party is,

that person, company or combination thereof, as the case may be.

(3) The Monetary Authority may, by notice in the Gazette, specify the factor for the purposes of subsection (2)(c), and any such notice may specify different factors for different items referred to in that subsection.

(4)   Where-

> *(a)*   the person referred to in subsection (1)(a) is a subsidiary or holding company of an authorized institution or a subsidiary of such holding company;

> *(b)*   the holding company referred to in subsection (1)(b)(i) is an authorized institution or a holding company of an authorized institution; or

> *(c)*   the holding company referred to in subsection (1)(c) is a holding company of an authorized institution,

the Monetary Authority may, by notice in writing to the institution, and subject to such conditions as he may think proper to attach thereto in any particular case, specify that subsection (1)(a), (b)(i) or (c), as the case may be, shall not apply for the purpose of determining the financial exposure of that institution and, accordingly, subsection (1)(a), (b)(i) or (c), as the case may be, shall not apply.

(4A)   Where-

> *(a)*   the holding company referred to in subsection (1)(b)(i) is The Financial Secretary Incorporated established under the Financial Secretary Incorporation Ordinance (Cap. 1015);

(b)   the controller referred to in subsection (1)(b)(ii) is the Government;

(c)   the holding company referred to in subsection (1)(c) is The Financial Secretary Incorporated; or

(d)   the controller referred to in subsection (1)(d) is the Government,

then subsection (1)(b)(i) or (ii), (c) or (d), as the case may be, shall not apply for the purpose of determining the financial exposure of the authorized institution concerned and, accordingly, that subsection shall not apply.

(5)   Where-

(a)   an authorized institution is financially exposed to a trustee in respect of 2 or more trusts; and

(b)   any person, company or combination thereof referred to in subsection (1)(a), (b), (c) or (d) is that trustee,

the Monetary Authority may, by notice in writing to the institution, and subject to such conditions as he may think proper to attach thereto in any particular case, specify that the financial exposure of that institution to that person, company or combination thereof, as the case may be, may exceed an amount equivalent to 25% of the capital base of the institution by an amount not more than the amount specified in that notice and, accordingly, such financial exposure of that institution may exceed the first-mentioned amount by an amount not more than the amount specified in that notice.

(6) For the purposes of this section, the financial exposure of an authorized institution shall not include-

(a)   any financial exposure to other authorized institutions;

(b)   any financial exposure to the extent to which it is-

     (i)   secured by-

         (A)   a cash deposit;

         (B)   a guarantee;
         (C)   another undertaking which, in the opinion of the Monetary Authority, is similar to a guarantee; or

> > **(D)** securities issued, or guaranteed, by the central government or the central bank of any Tier 1 country within the meaning of the Third Schedule; or
>
> **(ii)** covered by a letter of comfort,
>
> where such cash deposit, guarantee, other undertaking, securities or letter of comfort, as the case may be, is accepted by the Monetary Authority, and subject to such conditions as he may think proper to attach thereto, either generally or in any particular case;

(c) any financial exposure acquired by the purchase of bills of exchange or documents of title to goods where the holder of such bills or documents is entitled to payment outside Hong Kong for goods exported from Hong Kong;

(d) any advances, loans and credit facilities made against any bills or documents referred to in paragraph (c);

(e) any financial exposure to the Government;

(f) any financial exposure to any other government, except a government which is, in the opinion of the Monetary Authority, one that should not be accepted for the purposes of this section;

(g) any financial exposure to a bank incorporated outside Hong Kong which is not an authorized institution where any such bank is, in the opinion of the Monetary Authority, adequately supervised by the relevant banking supervisory authority;

(h) any share capital or debt securities held as security for facilities granted by the institution or, subject to subsection (7), acquired by it in the course of the satisfaction of debts due to it;

(i) any financial exposure acquired under an underwriting or sub underwriting contract-

> **(i)** where such financial exposure would, but for this subsection, be financial exposure under subsection (2)(b);
>
> **(ii)** for a period not exceeding 7 working days, or such further period as the Monetary Authority approves in

writing, and subject to such conditions as he may think proper to attach thereto in any particular case;

(j) any financial exposure acquired under an underwriting or subunderwriting contract where such financial exposure would, but for this subsection, be financial exposure under subsection (2)(c);

(k) any indemnity given by the institution to a person to protect that person against any damages which may be incurred by the person as a result of the person registering a transfer of shares where-

(i) the instrument by means of which the transfer has been effected, or purports to have been effected, has been provided, or purports to have been provided, by a subsidiary of the institution;

(ii) the authenticating signature on the instrument has been imprinted on it by a machine used by the subsidiary to imprint that signature on such instruments; and

(iii) that signature was unlawfully so imprinted on that instrument,

or any financial guarantee given by the institution to that person in respect of any like indemnity given by that subsidiary to that person;

(ka) any financial exposure to a multilateral development bank;

(kb) any financial exposure to the Housing Authority, within the meaning of the Housing Ordinance (Cap. 283), arising from guarantees it gives for the purposes of the Home Ownership Scheme or Private Sector Participation Scheme;

(l) any financial exposure to the extent to which it has been written off, or to which specific provision has been made for it, in the books of the institution.

(6A) The Financial Secretary may, by notice in the Gazette, amend subsection(6).

(7) All share capital and debt securities acquired by an authorized institution in the course of the satisfaction of debts due to it shall be disposed of at the earliest suitable opportunity, and in any event not later than 18 months after the acquisition thereof, or within such further period as the Monetary Authority approves in writing, and subject to such conditions as he may think proper to attach thereto, in any particular case.

(8) For the purposes of this section-

> *(a)* the expression "person" includes any partnership, any public body and any body of persons, corporate or unincorporate;

> *(b)* the expressions "debt securities" and "multilateral development bank" shall mean debt securities and multilateral development bank as respectively defined in paragraph 1 of the Third Schedule;

> *(c)* advances, loans, credit facilities, guarantees or liabilities shall be deemed to be granted to and to be outstanding in relation to any person liable or contingently liable thereon whether as principal debtor, guarantor, or otherwise:

Provided that the reference in this paragraph to a guarantor shall not include a person (not being an authorized institution) who guarantees the obligations of another under-

> **(i)** a hire purchase agreement, that is to say an agreement for the bailment of goods under which the bailee may buy the goods, or under which the property in the goods will or may pass to the bailee; or

> **(ii)** a conditional sale agreement, that is to say an agreement for the sale of goods under which the purchase price or part of it is payable by instalments, and the property in the goods is to remain in the seller (notwithstanding that the buyer is to be in possession of the goods) until such conditions as to payment of instalments or otherwise as may be specified in the agreement are fulfilled; and

> *(d)* a partnership of which an authorized institution is a member shall be deemed to be a subsidiary of that institution.

(9) Every director and every manager of an authorized institution which contravenes subsection (1) commits an offence and is liable-

> *(a)* on conviction upon indictment to a fine of $200,000 and to imprisonment for 2 years and, in the case of a continuing offence, to a further fine of $10,000 for every day during which the offence continues; or

(b)   on summary conviction to a fine of $50,000 and to imprisonment for 6 months and, in the case of a continuing offense, to a further fine of $5,000 for every day during which the offence continues.

Monetary Authority may publish guidelines on business practices of authorized institutions

82.(1) Without prejudice to section 7(3) or to the other provisions of this Part, the Monetary Authority may, after consultation with the Financial Secretary, by notice in the Gazette from time to time publish for the guidance of authorized institutions, guidelines, not inconsistent with this Ordinance, specifying business practices which should not be engaged in by authorized institutions because, in his opinion, such business practices will or may cause the soundness of the financial position of authorized institutions to be dependent upon the soundness of the financial position of a single party.

(2)   For the purposes of subsection (1), guidelines given in a notice under that

subsection-

(a)   may be expressed to apply to all authorized institutions or to a class of authorized institutions specified in the notice; and

(b)   may specify what constitutes a single party for the purposes of any such guidelines and, without prejudice to the generality of that power, any class or description of persons or business may constitute such a single party.

(3)   Where an authorized institution engages in business practices specified in a notice under subsection (1), the Monetary Authority, may, where he is of the opinion that the case is of sufficient importance to justify him so doing, exercise any of his powers under Part X in respect of the institution.

Limitations on advances to directors, etc. of bank

83.(1) Subject to subsection (4A), an authorized institution incorporated in HongKong shall not provide any facility specified in subsection (3) to or on behalf of any person or body specified in subsection (4) if the aggregate amount of such facilities for the time being provided by the institution to or on behalf of any one or more such persons or bodies would thereby exceed 10% of the capital base of the institution.

(2)   Subject to subsections (1) and (4A), an authorized institution incorporated in Hong Kong shall not provide any facility specified in subsection (3) to or on behalf of any person, being an individual, specified in subsection (4)(a), (b), (c), (d), (e) or (f) if the aggregate amount of such facilities for the time being provided by the institution to or on behalf of-

(a)   one or more such persons, would thereby exceed 5% of the capital base of the institution;

(b)   that person, would thereby exceed $1,000,000.

(3) Subject to subsection (3A), for the purposes of subsections (1) and (2), the following facilities are specified-

(a)   the granting, or permitting to be outstanding, of unsecured advances, unsecured loans or unsecured credit facilities including unsecured letters of credit;

(b)   the giving of unsecured financial guarantees; and

(c)   the incurring of any other unsecured liability.

(3A)   Subsection (3) shall not include any facility to the extent to which it has been written off, or to which specific provision has been made for it, in the books of the authorized institution concerned.

(4)   For the purposes of subsections (1) and (2), the following persons and bodies are specified-

(a)   any director of the institution;

(b)   any relative of any such director;

(c)   any employee of the institution who is responsible, either individually or as a member of a committee, for approving loan applications;

(d)   any relative of any such employee;

(e)   any controller or minority shareholder controller of the institution (other than an authorized institution, or a bank incorporated outside Hong Kong which is not an authorized institution but is approved by the Monetary Authority for the purposes of this paragraph);

(f)   any relative of an individual who is a controller or minority shareholder controller of the institution;

(g)   any firm, partnership or non-listed company (other than a firm, partnership or non-listed company which is an authorized institution, or a bank incorporated outside Hong Kong which is not an authorized institution but is approved by the Monetary Authority for the purposes of this paragraph) in which the institution or any of its controllers, minority shareholder controllers or directors or any relative of any of its controllers, minority shareholder controllers or directors is interested as director, partner, manager or agent; and

    (h)   any individual, firm, partnership or non-listed company of which any controller, minority shareholder controller or director of the institution or any relative of any such controller, minority shareholder controller or director is a guarantor.

(4A) The Monetary Authority may, by notice in writing to an authorized institution, and subject to such conditions as he may think proper to attach thereto in any particular case, permit the institution to grant, without complying with subsection (1) or (2), any facility specified in subsection (3) (or such of those facilities as he specifies in the notice) to or on behalf of any person or body specified in subsection (4) (or such of those persons or bodies as he specifies in the notice); and where the institution, in pursuance of such notice and in accordance with such conditions, grants any such facility to or on behalf of any such person or body it shall not thereby contravene subsection (1) or (2).

(5) The provisions of this section shall apply to a facility granted to or on behalf of a person or body jointly with another person or body as they apply to a facility granted to or on behalf of a person or body severally.

(6) For the purposes of subsections (2) and (4), a facility granted to or on behalf of any firm, partnership or non-listed company which a person specified in subsection (4)(a), (b), (c), (d), (e) or (f) is able to control, shall be deemed to be granted to that person or on his behalf.

(7) Every director and every manager of an authorized institution which contravenes subsection (1) or (2) commits an offence and is liable-

    (a)   on conviction upon indictment to a fine of $200,000 and to imprisonment for 2 years and, in the case of a continuing offence, to a further fine of $10,000 for every day during which the offence continues; or

    (b)   on summary conviction to a fine of $50,000 and to imprisonment for 6 months and, in the case of a continuing offence, to a further fine of $5,000 for every day during which the offence continues.

(8) Where, at any time before the commencement of the Banking (Amendment) Ordinance 1995, an authorized institution has lawfully provided a facility specified in subsection (3) to or on behalf of-

    (a)   a minority shareholder controller of the institution;

    (b)   any relative of such a controller;

    (c)   any firm, partnership or non-listed company in which such a controller or any relative of his is interested as director, partner, manager or agent; or

    (d)   any individual, firm, partnership or non-listed company of which such a controller or any relative of his is a guarantor,

then, in so far as that facility is concerned, this section shall operate as if the references to minority shareholder controller or minority shareholder controllers, as the case may be, in subsection (4)(e), (f), (g) and (h) were deleted.

84. *(Repealed)*

Limitation on advances to employees

85.(1) An authorized institution shall not provide to any one of its employees any facility specified in subsection (2) to an aggregate amount of such facilities in excess of one year's salary for the employee.

(2) For the purposes of subsection (1) the following facilities are specified-

    (a)   the granting, or permitting to be outstanding, of unsecured advances, unsecured loans or unsecured credit facilities including unsecured letters of credit;

    (b)   the giving of unsecured financial guarantees; and

    (c)   the incurring of any other unsecured liability.

(3) Every director and every manager of an authorized institution whichcontravenes this section commits an offence and is liable-

    (a)   on conviction upon indictment to a fine of $100,000 and to imprisonment for 12 months; or

    (b)   on summary conviction to a fine of $50,000 and to imprisonment for 6 months,

and, in the case of a continuing offence, to a further fine of $5,000 for every dayduring which the offense continues.

Powers of Monetary Authority where moneys placed with foreign bank

86.(1) Where the Monetary Authority-

(a) has reason to believe that an authorized institution has granted to any foreign bank any advances, loans (whether by way of deposit or otherwise) or credit facilities; and

(b) is of the opinion that the extent or manner in which such advances, loans or credit facilities have been made is not in the interests of the depositors of the authorized institution,

he may, by notice in writing to the institution, exercise his powers under this section.

(2) A notice under this section may-

(a) prohibit the authorized institution from granting, after the date of the service of the notice, any advances, loans or credit facilities to the foreign bank specified in the notice and any other foreign bank so specified which the Monetary Authority has reason to believe is associated with the first-mentioned foreign bank;

(b) where any moneys are held at call, demand or notice by the authorized institution with any bank specified by the Monetary Authority in pursuance of his powers under paragraph (a), direct the institution forthwith to demand repayment of such moneys in accordance with the terms upon which they are held;

(c) prohibit the authorized institution from permitting to be outstanding with any bank specified by the Monetary Authority in pursuance of his powers under paragraph (a)-

(i) any moneys which should have been repaid to the institution by virtue of a direction under paragraph (b);

(ii) any advances, loans or credit facilities repayable or terminable upon the elapse of any time or the occurrence of any event, after the elapse of such time or the occurrence of such event.

(3) A requirement under subsection (2)(a) shall not prohibit the grant of any advance or loan after the date of service of the notice in pursuance of any agreement entered into prior to such date unless the Monetary Authority otherwise directs; but it shall be the duty of the authorized institution to notify the Monetary Authority of any relevant agreement within 7 days of the receipt by it of a notice under this section.

(4) In this section-

"foreign bank" means-

    (a) any bank incorporated outside Hong Kong which is not an authorized institution;

    (b) any undertaking of an authorized institution, including that of the institution to which notice is given under this section, which is situated outside Hong Kong.

(5) Every director and every manager of an authorized institution which fails without reasonable excuse to comply with any requirement of the Monetary Authority in the exercise of his powers under this section commits an offence and is liable-

    (a) on conviction upon indictment to a fine of $200,000 and to imprisonment for 2 years and, in the case of a continuing offence, to a further fine of $10,000 for every day during which the offence continues; or

    (b) on summary conviction to a fine of $50,000 and to imprisonment for 6 months and, in the case of a continuing offence, to a further fine of $5,000 for every day during which the offence continues.

Limitation on shareholding by authorized institutions

87.(1) Subject to subsection (2), an authorized institution incorporated in HongKong shall not acquire or hold any part of the share capital of any other company or companies to an aggregate value in excess of 25 per cent of the capital base of the institution, except such share capital as the institution may hold as security for facilities granted by it or acquire in the course of the satisfaction of debts due to it:

    Provided that all share capital acquired in the course of the satisfaction of debts due to it shall be disposed of at the earliest suitable opportunity, and in any event not later than 18 months after the acquisition thereof or within such further period as the Monetary Authority approves in writing in any particular case.

(2) Subsection (1) shall not apply-

    (a) where an authorized institution acquires or holds any part of the share capital of any company or companies under an underwriting or subunderwriting contract for a period not

exceeding 7 working days, or such further period as the Monetary Authority approves in writing, and subject to such conditions as he may think proper to attach thereto, in any particular case;

(b) to any holding, approved in writing by the Monetary Authority, of share capital in-

(i) another authorized institution; or

(ii) a company carrying out nominee, executor or trustee functions, or other functions related to banking business, the business of taking deposits, insurance business, investments or other financial services; or

(c) to any holding, approved in writing by the Monetary Authority, of share capital which is deducted in determining the capital base of the authorized institution.

(3) Every director and every manager of an authorized institution whichcontravenes this section commits an offence and is liable-

(a) on conviction upon indictment to a fine of $200,000 and to imprisonment for 2 years and, in the case of a continuing

offence, to a further fine of $10,000 for every day during which the offence continues; or

(b) on summary conviction to a fine of $50,000 and to imprisonment for 6 months and, in the case of a continuing offence, to a further fine of $5,000 for every day during which the offence continues.

(4) *(Repealed)*

Limitation on holding of interest in land by authorized institutions

88.(1) An authorized institution incorporated in Hong Kong shall not purchase or hold any interest or interests in land situated in or outside Hong Kong of a value or to an aggregate value, as the case may be, in excess of 25 per cent of the capital base of the institution.

(2) An authorized institution may, in addition to the value of any land permitted to be purchased or held under subsection (1), purchase or hold interests in land situated in or outside Hong Kong to any value, where the occupation of such land is, in the opinion of the Monetary Authority, necessary for conducting the business of the institution or providing housing or amenities for the staff of the institution.

(3) For the purposes of subsection (2), but without limiting the generality thereof, the Monetary Authority may in his discretion regard as necessary for conducting the business of an authorized institution the whole of any premises in which an office of the institution is situated.

(4) (*Repealed*)

(5) There shall not be taken into account in the assessment of the valueof interests in land for the purposes of this section the value of any interest in land mortgaged to the authorized institution to secure a debt due to the institution nor the value of any interest in land acquired pursuant to entry into possession of land so mortgaged, provided that the interest acquired is disposed of at the earliest suitable opportunity, and in any event not later than 18 months after its acquisition or within such further period as the Monetary Authority may, in writing, allow in any particular case.

(6) Every director and every manager of an authorized institution which contravenes this section commits an offense and is liable-

- (a) on conviction upon indictment to a fine of $200,000 and to imprisonment for 2 years and, in the case of a continuing offence, to a further fine of $ 1 0,000 for every day during which the offence continues; or

- (b) on summary conviction to a fine of $50,000 and to imprisonment for 6 months and, in the case of a continuing offence, to a further fine of $5,000 for every day during which the offence continues.

89. (*Repealed*)

Limitation on aggregate holdings under sections 83, 87 and 88

90.(1) Notwithstanding anything contained in sections 83, 87 and 88, in respect of an authorized institution, the aggregate total of-

- (a) the amount outstanding of all facilities specified in section 83(3) provided to or on behalf of persons or bodies specified in section 83(4);

- (b) the value of all holdings of share capital specified in section 87; and

- (c) the value of all holdings of interests in land specified in section 88(1) and (2),

shall not at any time exceed 80% of the capital base of the institution.

(2) In assessing the aggregate total which is permissible under subsection (1) there shall not be taken into account any matter which is excluded from the operation of section 83, 87 or 88 by virtue of any of the provisions thereof unless the Monetary Authority, by notice in writing to the authorized institution concerned, otherwise specifies.

(3) Every director and every manager of an authorized institution which contravenes this section commits an offence and is liable-

> *(a)* on conviction upon indictment to a fine of $200,000 and to imprisonment for 2 years and, in the case of a continuing offence, to a further fine of $10,000 for every day during which the offence continues; or

> *(b)* on summary conviction to a fine of $50,000 and to imprisonment for 6 months and, in the case of a continuing offence, to a further fine of $5,000 for every day during which the offence continues.

Proof of compliance with section 80, 81, 83, 85, 86, 87, 88 or 90

91.(1) Any authorized institution, if at any time called upon in writing by the Monetary Authority so to do, shall satisfy him by the production of such evidence or information as he may require, that the institution is not in contravention of any of the provisions of section 80, 81, 83, 85, 86, 87, 88 or 90 applicable to that institution.

(2) Any authorized institution, if at any time called upon in writing by the Monetary Authority so to do, shall satisfy him by the production of such evidence or information as he may require, whether or not the institution is engaging in any business practices specified in a notice under section 82.

(3) Every director and every manager of an authorized institution which fails or refuses without reasonable excuse to comply with subsection (1) or (2) commits an offence and is liable-

> *(a)* on conviction upon indictment to a fine of $200,000 and to imprisonment for 2 years and, in the case of a continuing offense, to a further fine of $10,000 for every day during which the offence continues; or

> *(b)* on summary conviction to a fine of $50,000 and to imprisonment for 6 months and, in the case of a continuing offence, to a further fine of $5,000 for every day during which the offence continues.

PART XVI - Advertisements, Representations And Use Of

Title "Bank"

Offence to issue advertisements and documents relating to deposits

92.(1) Subject to subsection (5), no person shall-

    (a) issue, or have in his possession for the purposes of issue, any advertisement which to his knowledge is or contains an invitation to members of the public-

        (i) to make any deposit; or

        (ii) to enter into, or offer to enter into, any agreement to make any deposit;

    (b) issue, or have in his possession for the purposes of issue, any document which to his knowledge contains such an advertisement; or

    (c in any other manner issue or make an invitation to members of the public to do any of the acts referred to in paragraph (a).

(2) Any person who contravenes subsection (1) commits an offence and is liable on conviction upon indictment or on summary conviction to a fine of $10,000.

(3) For the purposes of any proceedings under this section, an advertisement or document in which a person named in the advertisement or document holds himself out as being prepared to take in Hong Kong any deposit shall, subject to subsection (4), be presumed, unless such named person proves to the contrary, to have been issued by him.

(4) A person shall not be taken to contravene this section by reason only that he issues, or has in his possession for the purposes of issue, to purchasers copies of any newspaper, magazine, journal or other periodical publication of general and regular circulation, which contain an advertisement to which this section applies.

(4A) For the purposes of any proceedings under this section, a person whose business it is to publish or arrange for the publication of advertisements shall not be taken to contravene this section if he proves that-

    (a) he received the advertisement for publication in the ordinary course of his business;

    (b) the matters contained in the advertisement were not (wholly or

in part) devised or selected by him or by any person under his direction or control; and

(c)   he did not know and had no reason for believing that publication of the advertisement would constitute an offence.

(5) This section shall not apply to-

(a)   any advertisement or invitation, or any document containing any advertisement or invitation, to make a deposit or to enter into, or offer to enter into, any agreement to make a deposit with an authorized institution;

(b)   any advertisement or invitation, or any document containing any advertisement or invitation, to which section 4(1) of the Protection of Investors Ordinance (Cap. 335) does not apply by virtue of section 4(2)(fb), (fc), (g) or (h) of that Ordinance; or

(c)   any prescribed advertisement which complies with the requirements specified in the Fifth Schedule applicable to the prescribed advertisement.

(6) Where any advertisement or invitation, or any document containing any advertisement or invitation, relates to the taking of any deposit and the taking of any such deposit is not, by virtue of section 3(1) or (2), a taking to which Part III applies then, to the extent that such advertisement, invitation or document, as the case may be, relates to the taking of any such deposit, this section shall not apply to such advertisement, invitation or document, as the case may be.

(7) In this section and the Fifth Schedule, "prescribed advertisement" means any advertisement or invitation, or any document containing any advertisement or invitation, to make a deposit or to enter into, or offer to enter into, any agreement to make a deposit outside Hong Kong.

Fraudulent inducement to make a deposit

93.(1) Any person who, by any fraudulent or reckless misrepresentation, induces another person-

(a)   to make a deposit with him or any other person; or

(b)   to enter into or to offer to enter into any agreement to make a deposit with him or any other person,

commits an offence and is liable on conviction upon indictment to a fine of $1,000,000 and to imprisonment for 7 years.

(2) For the purposes of subsection (1), "fraudulent or reckless misrepresentation" means-

    (a)   any statement-

        (i)   which, to the knowledge of the maker of the statement, was false, misleading or deceptive; or

        (ii)   which was false, misleading or deceptive and was made recklessly;

    (b)   any promise-

        (i)   which the maker of the promise had no intention of fulfilling;

        (ii)   which, to the knowledge of the maker of the promise, was not capable of being fulfilled; or

        (iii)   which was made recklessly;

    (c)   any forecast-

        (i)   which, to the knowledge of the maker of the forecast, was not justified on the basis of facts known to him at the time when he made it; or

        (ii)   which was not justified on the facts known to the maker of the forecast at the time when he made it and was made recklessly; or

    (d)   any statement or forecast from which the maker intentionally or recklessly omitted a material fact with the result that the statement or forecast was thereby rendered false, misleading or deceptive.

Liability in tort for inducing persons to make a deposit in certain cases

94.(1) Any person who, by any fraudulent, reckless or negligent misrepresentation, induces another person to make a deposit with him or any other person shall be liable to pay compensation to the person so induced for any pecuniary loss that such person has sustained by reason of his reliance on that misrepresentation.

(2) For the purposes of subsection (1), "fraudulent, reckless or negligent misrepresentation" means-

(a) any statement-

    (i) which, to the knowledge of the maker of the statement, was false, misleading or deceptive;

    (ii) which was false, misleading or deceptive and was made recklessly; or

    (iii) which was false, misleading or deceptive and was made without reasonable care having been taken to ensure its accuracy;

(b) any promise-

    (i) which the maker of the promise had no intention of fulfilling;

    (ii) which, to the knowledge of the maker of the promise, was not capable of being fulfilled; or

    (iii) which was made recklessly or without reasonable care having been taken to ensure that it could be fulfilled;

(c) any forecast-

    (i) which, to the knowledge of the maker of the forecast, was not justified on the basis of facts known to him at the time when he made it; or

    (ii) which was not justified on the facts known to the maker of the forecast at the time when he made it and was made recklessly or without reasonable care having been taken to ascertain the accuracy of those facts; or

(d) any statement or forecast from which the maker intentionally, recklessly or negligently omitted a material fact with the result that the statement or forecast was thereby rendered false, misleading or deceptive.

(3) For the purposes of this section, where any statement, promise or forecast to which this section relates was made by a company, every person who was a director or controller of the company at the time when the statement, promise or forecast was made shall, until the contrary is proved, be deemed to have caused or permitted it to be made.

(4) This section does not affect any liability of any person at common law.

(5) An action may be brought under this section notwithstanding that the evidence on which the action is or will be based, if substantiated, discloses the commission of an offence and no person has been charged with or convicted of the offence.

(6) For the purposes of this section "company" means, in addition to a company as defined in section 2, any other body of persons, corporate or unincorporate.

False, etc. advertisements by authorized institution

95.(1) Where the Monetary Authority is of the opinion that any advertisement issued in connexion with the business of an authorized institution makes a statement or any representation that is false, misleading or deceptive, he may, by notice in writing served on the institution, require the institution to withdraw or, as the circumstances require, remove, and to cease issuing such advertisements and an authorized institution served with such a notice shall, accordingly, comply with that notice.

(2) Any authorized institution aggrieved by a notice served under subsection (1) may appeal to the Financial Secretary against the requirement contained therein, but the notice shall take effect immediately notwithstanding that an appeal has been or may be made under this subsection.

(3) Every director and every manager of an authorized institution which fails or refuses to comply with any notice served under this section on it commits an offence and is liable-

> *(a)* on conviction upon indictment to a fine of $200,000 and to imprisonment for 2 years and, in the case of a continuing offence, to a further fine of $10,000 for every day during which the offence continues; or

> *(b)* on summary conviction to a fine of $50,000 and to imprisonment for 6 months and, in the case of a continuing offence, to a further fine of $5,000 for every day during which the offence continues.

Certain representations prohibited

96.(1) An authorized institution shall not in any communication, whether written or oral, represent or imply, or permit to be represented or implied, in any manner to any person that the institution has in any respect been approved by the Government, the Financial Secretary or the Monetary Authority.

(2) Subsection (1) is not contravened by reason only that a statement is made to the effect that an authorized institution is authorized.

(3) Every director and every manager of an authorized institution which contravenes subsection (1) without reasonable excuse commits an offence and is liable-

(a)   on conviction upon indictment to a fine of $200,000 and to imprisonment for 2 years; or

(b)   on summary conviction to a fine of $50,000 and to imprisonment for 6 months.

Restrictions on use of name "bank"

97.(1) Subject to this section, any person, other than a bank, or an institution which is recognized as the central bank of the place in which it is incorporated, who, without the written consent of the Monetary Authority given generally or in any particular case or class of case-

(a)   uses the word "bank" or any of its derivatives in English, or any translation thereof in any language or uses the Chinese expression "ngan hong", or uses the letters "b", "a" , "n" , "k" in that order, in the description or name under which such person is carrying on business in Hong Kong; or

(b)   makes any representation in any bill head, letter paper, notice, advertisement or in any other manner whatsoever that such person is a bank or is carrying on banking business in Hong Kong,

commits an offence and is liable-

(i)   on conviction upon indictment to a fine of $200,000 and to imprisonment for 12 months; or

(ii)   on summary conviction to a fine of $50,000 and to imprisonment for 6 months.

(1A)   Where a bank-

(a)-(b) (*Repealed*)

(c)   uses, in the name under which it carries on business as a bank in the place where it is incorporated, any of the terms to which subsection (1)(a) applies,

nothing in subsection (1)(a) shall prohibit a local representative office of the bank from using the same name, or any translation thereof in any language, in the name under which the representative office is carrying on in Hong Kong the functions and activities of a representative office provided such name-

    (i)   is used in immediate conjunction with the term "representative office" in the same language as such name (which term, in the case of Chinese, shall be the characters; and

    (ii)   is not more prominent than such term.

(1B) *(Repealed)*

(2) Nothing in this section shall apply to any association of banks formed for the protection or promotion of their mutual interests or to any association of employees of banks formed for the protection or promotion of the mutual interests of such employees.

(3) Nothing in subsection (1)(a) shall prohibit a restricted licence bank using a specified term in the description under which the restricted licence bank is carrying on in Hong Kong the business of taking deposits.

(4)   Where a restricted licence bank-

    (a)   is incorporated outside Hong Kong;

    (b)   is a bank in the place where it is incorporated; and

    (c)   uses, in the name under which it carries on business as a bank in the place where it is incorporated, any of the terms to which subsection (1)(a) applies,

nothing in subsection (1)(a) shall prohibit the restricted licence bank from using the same name, or any translation thereof in any language, in the name under which the restricted licence bank is carrying on in Hong Kong the business of taking deposits provided such name-

    (i)   is used in immediate conjunction with the term "restricted licence bank" in the same language as such name (which term, in the case of Chinese, shall be the characters specified in paragraph (a) of the definition of "specified term" in subsection (6)); and

    (ii)   is not more prominent than such term.

(5)   Nothing in this Ordinance shall affect the determination of any question whether a restricted licence bank or a deposit-taking company is a bank for purposes other than those of this Ordinance, and accordingly nothing in this section shall prohibit a restricted licence bank or a deposit-taking company from using any of the terms to which subsection (1)(a) applies with reference to itself in any case where-

(a)   it wishes to comply with or take advantage of any relevant provision of law or custom; and

(b)   it is necessary for it to use any such term in order to be able to assert that it is complying with or entitled to take advantage of that provision.

(6)   In this section-

"description" includes any statement (whether or not in writing) which uses any of the terms to which subsection (1)(a) applies where that statement may be construed to mean that a person (howsoever described) is-

(a)   a subsidiary;

(b)   the holding company; or

(c)   a subsidiary of the holding company,

of a bank (and whether or not such bank is authorized or exists);

"relevant provision of law or custom" means any enactment, any instrument made under an enactment, any international agreement, any rule of law or any commercial usage or practice which confers any benefit on, or otherwise has effect only in relation to, a person by virtue of such person being a bank;

"specified term" means any of the following terms-

(a)   "restricted licence bank";

(b)   "merchant bank";

(c)   "investment bank";

(d)   "wholesale bank";

(e)   a term specified by the Monetary Authority by notice in the Gazette to be a specified term for the purposes of this definition,

and includes any derivatives of those terms in English or Chinese.

(7) Where, immediately before the commencement of the Banking (Amendment) Ordinance 1995, a company was lawfully exercising the privilege conferred upon it under subsection (1B) as in force immediately before that commencement, then the company may continue to exercise that privilege as if-

(a)   that subsection had not been repealed but the word "name" had been substituted for the word "title" in paragraph (a) of that subsection; and

(b)   the definition of "specified bank" in subsection (6) as in force immediately before that commencement had not been repealed but the word "authorized" had been substituted for the words "licensed under section 16" in paragraphs (a) and (b)(i) of that definition.

False statements as to authorized status

97A.(1)   No person shall describe himself, or otherwise hold himself out, so as to indicate, or reasonably be construed to indicate, that he is-

(a)   an authorized institution, or carrying on in Hong Kong the business of taking deposits, unless he is an authorized institution;

(b)   a bank, or carrying on in Hong Kong banking business, unless he is a bank;

(c)   a restricted licence bank unless he is a restricted licence bank;

(d)   a deposit-taking company unless he is a deposit-taking company; or

(e)   a local representative office unless he is a local representative office.

(2)   Any person who contravenes subsection (1) commits an offence and is liable-

(a)   on conviction upon indictment to a fine of $200,000 and to imprisonment for 2 years; or

(b)   on summary conviction to a fine of $50,000 and to imprisonment for 6 months.

PART XVII - Capital Adequacy Ratio Of Authorized Institutions

Capital adequacy ratio

98.(1) Subject to this Part and Part X, an authorized institution incorporated in Hong Kong shall not, at any time, have a capital adequacy ratio of less than 8 per ent as calculated in accordance with the provisions of the Third Schedule and subsection (2) except that any requirement under section 79A(1) referred to in that Schedule shall not apply in calculating such capital adequacy ratio.

(2) Subject to subsection (2A), for the purposes of calculating the capital adequacy ratio of an authorized institution which has any subsidiary, the Monetary Authority may, by notice in writing to the institution, require the capital adequacy ratio of the institution to be calculated-

> *(a)*   on a consolidated basis instead of on an unconsolidated basis; or

> *(b)*   on both a consolidated basis and an unconsolidated basis.

(2A) The Monetary Authority may, in a notice under subsection (2) to an authorized institution, require the capital adequacy ratio of the institution to be calculated on a consolidated basis only in respect of such subsidiaries of the institution as are specified in the notice.

(3) The Financial Secretary may, by notice in the Gazette, vary the percentage specified in subsection (1).

Failure to keep to capital adequacy ratio

99.(1) Where an authorized institution contravenes section 98(1), it shall forthwith notify the Monetary Authority of that contravention and provide him with such particulars of that contravention as he may require.

(2) Where the Monetary Authority is notified under subsection (1) of a contravention of section 98(1), he shall forthwith notify the Financial Secretary of that contravention and provide him with such particulars of that contravention as he may require.

(3) Every director and every manager of an authorized institution which contravenes subsection (1) commits an offense and is liable on conviction upon indictment to a fine of $500,000 and to imprisonment for 5 years and, in the case of a continuing offence, to a further fine of $10,000 for every day during which the offence continues.

Remedial action

100.(1) Where an authorized institution contravenes section 98(1), the institution and the Monetary Authority shall enter into discussions for the purposes of determining what remedial action is required to be taken by the institution for it to comply with that section, but the Monetary Authority shall not be bound by any such discussions.

(2) The Monetary Authority may, after holding such discussions as he thinks fit under subsection (1), by notice in writing served on the authorized institution, require the institution to take such remedial action as is specified in the notice for the purpose of having the institution comply with section 98(1).

(3) Any authorized institution aggrieved by any requirement contained in a notice under subsection (2) served on it by the Monetary Authority may appeal to the Governor in Council against the requirement, but that requirement shall take effect immediately, notwithstanding that an appeal has been or may be made under this subsection.

(4) (*Repealed*)

(5) Every director and every manager of an authorized institution which contravenes any requirement contained in a notice under subsection (2) commits an offence and is liable on conviction upon indictment to a fine of $500,000 and to imprisonment for 5 years and, in the case of a continuing offence, to a further fine of $10,000 for every day during which the offence continues.

Monetary Authority may increase capital adequacy

ratio for particular authorized institutions

101.(1) The Monetary Authority may, after consultation with an authorized institution, by notice in writing served on it vary the capital adequacy ratio specified in section 98(1) in relation to that institution by increasing the ratio to-

> *(a)* in the case of an authorized institution which is a bank, not more than 12 per cent; and

> *(b)* in the case of an authorized institution which is a deposit-taking company or a restricted licence bank, not more than 16 per cent,

and, where the ratio is so varied, the other provisions of this Part shall, in relation to that institution, apply as if the ratio specified in section 98(1) were the ratio as so varied.

) The Financial Secretary may, by notice in the Gazette, vary any percentage specified in subsection (1).

(3) An authorized institution aggrieved by a variation of the capital adequacy ratio contained in a notice under subsection (1) served on it by the Monetary Authority may appeal to the Governor in Council against the variation, but that variation shall take effect immediately, notwithstanding that the appeal has been or may be made under this subsection.

(4) (*Repealed*)

PART XVIII - Liquidity Ratio Of Authorized Institutions And

Matters Affecting Liquidity Ratio

Liquidity ratio

102.(1) Subject to this Part and Part X, every authorized institution shall maintain a liquidity ratio of not less than 25 per cent in each calendar month as calculated in accordance with the provisions of the Fourth Schedule and this Part.

(2)   (*Repealed*)

(3) Subject to subsection (3A), in relation to an authorized institutionthat operates in Hong Kong and also elsewhere, this Part shall apply only to its principal place of business in Hong Kong and its local branches and shall do so as if that principal place of business and those branches were collectively a separate authorized institution.

(3A)   Subject to subsection (3B), for the purposes of calculating the liquidity ratio of an authorized institution incorporated in Hong Kong, the Monetary Authority may, by notice in writing to the institution, require the liquidity ratio of the institution to be calculated-

> *(a)*   on a consolidated basis instead of an unconsolidated basis; or

> *(b)*   on both a consolidated basis and an unconsolidated basis.

(3B) The Monetary Authority may, in a notice under subsection (3A) to an authorized institution, require the liquidity ratio of the institution to be calculated on a consolidated basis only in respect of such subsidiaries and overseas branches of the institution as are specified in the notice.

(3C) For the avoidance of doubt, it is hereby declared that the calculation of the liquidity ratio of an authorized institution on an unconsolidated basis means that any subsidiaries or overseas branches of the institution are excluded for the purposes of that calculation.

(4) The Financial Secretary may, by notice in the Gazette, vary the percentage specified in subsection (1).

Failure to keep to liquidity ratio

103.(1) Where an authorized institution contravenes section 102(1), it shall forthwith notify the Monetary Authority of that contravention and provide him with such particulars of that contravention as he may require.

(2) Where the Monetary Authority is notified under subsection (1) of a contravention of section 102(1), he shall forthwith notify the Financial Secretary of that contravention and provide him with such particulars of that contravention as he may require.

(3) Every director and every manager of an authorized institution which contravenes subsection (1) commits an offence and is liable on conviction upon indictment to a fine of $500,000 and to imprisonment for 5 years and, in the case of a continuing offence, to a further fine of $10,000 for every day during which the offence continues.

Remedial action

104.(1) Where an authorized institution contravenes section 102(1), the institution and the Monetary Authority shall enter into discussions for the purposes of determining what remedial action is required to be taken by the institution for it to comply with that section, but the Monetary Authority shall not be bound by any such discussions.

(2) The Monetary Authority may, after holding such discussions as he thinks fit under subsection (1), by notice in writing served on the authorized institution, require the institution to take such remedial action as is specified in the notice for the purpose of having the institution comply with section 102(1).

(3) Any authorized institution aggrieved by any requirement contained in a notice under subsection (2) served on it by the Monetary Authority may appeal to the Governor in Council against the requirement, but that requirement shall take effect immediately, notwithstanding that an appeal has been or may be made under this subsection.

(4) (*Repealed*)

(5) Every director and every manager of an authorized institution whichcontravenes any requirement contained in a notice under subsection (2) commits an offence and is liable on conviction upon indictment to a fine of $500,000 and to imprisonment for 5 years and, in the case of a continuing offence, to a further fine of $10,000 for every day during which the offence continues.

Monetary Authority may vary liquidity ratio for particular authorized institutions

105.(1) The Monetary Authority may, by notice in writing served on an authorized institution, vary the liquidity ratio specified in section 102(1) in relation to that institution by increasing or decreasing the ratio and, where the ratio is so varied, sections 102, 103 and 104 shall, in relation to that institution, apply as if the ratio specified in section 102(1) were the ratio as so varied.

(2) Where the Monetary Authority varies under subsection (1) the liquidity ratio of any authorized institution, he shall forthwith provide the Financial Secretary with particulars of the variation.

(3) An authorized institution aggrieved by a variation of the liquidity ratio contained in a notice under subsection (1) served on it by the Monetary Authority may appeal to the Governor in Council against the variation, but that variation shall take effect immediately, notwithstanding that an appeal has been or may be made under this subsection.

(4) (*Repealed*)

Authorized institutions not to create certain
charges and to notify Monetary Authority of certain civil proceedings

106.(1) An authorized institution incorporated in Hong Kong shall not, except with the approval of the Monetary Authority, which approval shall be subject to such conditions as he may think proper to attach thereto, by whatever means create any charge over its assets if either-

(a) the aggregate value of all charges existing over its total assets (excluding contra items) is 5% or more of the value of those total assets; or

(b) creating that charge would cause the aggregate value of all charges (including that first-mentioned charge) over its total assets (excluding contra items) to be more than 5% of the value of those total assets.

(2) The Monetary Authority may, by notice in the Gazette, specify a charge, or a class of charges, to which subsection (1) shall not apply.

(3) Where any civil proceedings have been instituted against any authorized institution incorporated in Hong Kong, irrespective of whether the proceedings have been instituted before, on or after the commencement of this Ordinance, the institution shall, if those proceedings materially affect, or could materially affect, the financial position of the institution, forthwith notify the Monetary Authority of those proceedings and provide the Monetary Authority with such particulars of those proceedings as he may require.

(4) Every director and every manager of an authorized institution which contravenes subsection (1) or (3) commits an offense and is liable-

(a) on conviction upon indictment to a fine of $200,000 and to imprisonment for 2 years and, in the case of a continuing offence, to a further fine of $10,000 for every day during which the offence continues; and

(b) on summary conviction to a fine of $50,000 and to imprisonment for 6 months and, in the case of a continuing offence, to a further fine of $5,000 for every day during which the offence continues.

(5) For the purposes of subsection (1) -

"assets" includes assets outside Hong Kong;

"charge" includes lien, encumbrance, equitable interest and third party right, but does not include a charge, or a class of charges, specified in a notice under subsection (2);
"value" shall have the same meaning assigned to it in section 79(1).

PART XIX

107-116. (*Repealed*)

PART XX - Investigations Of Authorized Institutions

Investigations on behalf of Financial Secretary

117.(1) If it appears to the Monetary Authority that it is in the interests of depositors of an authorized institution or a former authorized institution or in the public interest that an inquiry should be made into the affairs, business or property of that institution he may make a report to that effect to the Financial Secretary.

(2) The Financial Secretary, on receipt of a report under subsection (1), may appoint a competent person to report to him and the Monetary Authority on the state and conduct of the affairs, business and property of the authorized institution or former authorized institution concerned, or any particular aspect thereof specified by the Financial Secretary.

(3) The Financial Secretary may, from time to time after making an appointment under subsection (2), and before the person so appointed reports to him, require that person to inquire into any further aspect of the authorized institution or former authorized institution concerned.

(4) The person appointed under subsection (2) shall be paid such remuneration and allowances and be appointed on such terms as the Financial Secretary shall from time to time determine.

(5) On receipt of the report of the person appointed under subsection (2) the Financial Secretary may, without limiting the generality of the exercise by him of any other powers which he may exercise under this Ordinance-

> (a)   if he is of the opinion that it is in the public interest to do so, cause the whole or any part of a report under this section to be published in such manner as he thinks fit:

Provided that nothing in a report published under this paragraph shall enable any particular customer of an authorized institution to be identified or reveal details of the affairs of any such customer without the consent of that customer;

> (b)   require the person appointed under subsection (2) to report further on any matters arising from the report;

> (c)   refer the report to the Governor in Council with the

recommendation that the Governor in Council should exercise his power under section 53(1)(iii);

(d)   if it appears that an offence may have been committed by any person, refer the report to the Attorney General;

(e)   (*Repealed*)

(f)   apply to the High Court for a winding-up order under section 122(5).

(6) The Financial Secretary shall not exercise his powers under subsection(2) in the case of a former authorized institution which ceased to be an authorized institution 12 months or more before the date of the report under subsection (1).

(7) Any person who-

(a)   with intent to defeat the purposes of this section or to delay or obstruct the carrying out of an investigation under this section-

(i)   conceals, destroys, mutilates or alters a document relating to a matter which is the subject of an investigation by a person appointed under subsection (2); or

(ii)   sends, or causes to be sent, or conspires with another person to send, out of Hong Kong any such document; or

(b)   knowingly furnishes to a person appointed under subsection (2) any information which is false or misleading in a material particular,

commits an offence and is liable on conviction upon indictment or on summary conviction to a fine of $20,000 and to imprisonment for 2 years.

(8) For the avoidance of doubt, it is hereby declared that the reference in subsection (6) to "former authorized institution" shall include any person which was a deposit-taking company within the meaning of this Ordinance as in force at any time before the commencement of the Banking (Amendment) Ordinance 1990.

Powers of the inspector and offences in connection with the investigation

118.(1) Subject to this section, the inspector may determine the manner in which an inquiry under section 117 is to proceed.

(2) If the inspector thinks it necessary for the purposes of his investigation, he may also investigate the affairs, business and property of any company which is or has at any relevant time been-

  (a)   a holding company or subsidiary of the body whose affairs, business and property is under investigation;

  (b)   a subsidiary of a holding company of that body; or

  (c)   a holding company of a subsidiary of that body.

(3) It shall be the duty of every director, manager, employee, or agent of a company whose affairs, business and property is under investigation (whether by virtue of section 117(2) or subsection (2)) and any person who has in his possession books, papers or information relevant to the investigation-

  (a)   to produce to the inspector all books and papers relating to the company concerned which are in his custody or power;

  (b)   to attend before the inspector when required to do so; and

  (c)   to answer truthfully and to the best of his ability any questions which may be put to him by the inspector and which are relevant to the investigation:

Provided that an inspector shall not require the disclosure by a solicitor or counsel of any privileged communication, whether oral or written, made to or by him in that capacity.

(4) Anything said by any person in answer to a question put by the inspector under subsection (3)(c) shall be inadmissible in any criminal proceedings other than criminal proceedings brought under this section.

(5) Any director, manager, employee or agent of a company and any other person who-

  (a)   without reasonable excuse fails to produce any books or papers which it is his duty to produce under subsection (3); or

  (b)   without reasonable excuse fails to attend before the inspector when required to do so under this section; or

  (c)   fails to answer to the best of his ability any question which is put to him by an inspector with respect to any affairs, business and property which are or is under investigation under section 117 or to the affairs, business and property of any body corporate which are or is being investigated by virtue of subsection (2)

commits an offence and is liable on conviction upon indictment or on summary conviction to a fine of $20,000 and to imprisonment for 6 months.

(6)   In this section-

        (a)   "inspector" means a person appointed under section 117(2);

        (b)   any reference to a director, manager, employee or agent of a company includes a reference to a person who has been but no longer is a director, manager, employee or agent of that company;

        (c)   "agent" in relation to a company whose affairs, business and property are or is under investigation includes its bankers and solicitors and any persons, whether officers of the body or not, who are employed as its auditors.

PART XXI - Miscellaneous

Governor in Council to decide whether or not banking business or business

of taking deposits is being conducted

119.(1) In the event of any dispute as to whether a person is carrying on a banking business or a business of taking deposits, the matter, except in the case of a prosecution for any offence against this Ordinance, shall be submitted to the Governor in Council for his determination; and the decision of the Governor in Council shall be final and conclusive for all purposes of this Ordinance.

(2) A submission under subsection (1) may be made by the Financial Secretary or by any bank, deposit-taking company or restricted licence bank or person which or who is interested in the determination of the matter.

Official secrecy

120.(1) Except as may be necessary for the exercise of any function under this Ordinance or for carrying into effect the provisions of this Ordinance, every person to whom this subsection applies-

    (a)   shall preserve and aid in preserving secrecy with regard to all matters relating to the affairs of any person that may come to his knowledge in the exercise of any function under this Ordinance;

    (b)   shall not communicate any such matter to any person other than the person to whom such matter relates; and

    (c)   shall not suffer or permit any person to have access to any records in the possession, custody or control of any person to whom this subsection applies.

(2) Subsection (1) shall apply to any person who is or has been-

    (a)   a public officer;

    (b)   a person authorized by the Monetary Authority;

    (c)   the Advisor of an authorized institution;

    (d)   the Manager of an authorized institution;

    (da)   a person appointed under section 53G(5);

(e)   a person appointed under section 117(2); and

(f)   a person employed by or assisting a person to whom this subsection applies by virtue of paragraph (b), (c), (d), or (e),

who exercises or has exercised any function under this Ordinance.

(3) Subsection (1) shall not apply if the Manager of an authorized institution is required to comply with a notice to furnish returns and information under section 51 of the Inland Revenue Ordinance (Cap. 112).

(4) No person who exercises any function in the course of an examination or investigation under section 47, 50, 55 or 117 or who receives reports, returns or information submitted under section 47, 50, 55, 56, 59, 63 or 64 shall be required to produce in any court any book, account or other document whatsoever or to divulge or communicate to any court any matter or thing coming under his notice in the exercise of his functions under this Ordinance, except as may be necessary in the course of a prosecution for any offence or of a winding-up by the High Court under section 122.

(5) Subsection (1) shall not apply-

(a)   to the disclosure of information in the form of a summary of similar information provided by a number of authorized institutions if the summary is so framed as to prevent particulars relating to the business of any particular authorized institution being ascertained from it;

(b)   to the disclosure of information with a view to the institution of, or otherwise for the purposes of, any criminal proceedings, whether under this Ordinance or otherwise;

(c)   in connection with any other legal proceedings arising out of this Ordinance;

(d)   to the disclosure of information to the police or the Independent Commission Against Corruption, at the request of the Attorney General, relevant to the proper investigation of any criminal complaint;

(e)   to the disclosure of information by the Monetary Authority with a view to the institution of, or otherwise for the purposes of, any disciplinary proceedings relating to the exercise of his

professional duties by an auditor or former auditor of an authorized institution or former authorized institution, whether or not the auditor or former auditor, as the case may be, was appointed under section 50, 59 or 63;

(f)   to the disclosure of information by the Monetary Authority to the Governor, the Financial Secretary, the Secretary for Financial Services, an inspector appointed by the Financial Secretary to investigate the affairs of a company, a person holding an authorized statutory office or any public officer authorized by the Financial Secretary for the purposes of this paragraph where, in the opinion of the Monetary Authority

         (i)   it is desirable or expedient that information should be so disclosed in the interests of depositors or potential depositors or the public interest; or

         (ii)   such disclosure will enable or assist the recipient of the information to exercise his functions and it is not contrary to the interests of depositors or potential depositors or the public interest that the information should be so disclosed;

(g)   to the disclosure of information by the Monetary Authority to an auditor of an authorized institution or former authorized institution, or to a former auditor, for the purpose of enabling or assisting the Monetary Authority to discharge his functions under this Ordinance;

(ga)   to the disclosure of information-

         (i)   to any person appointed under section 5A(3) of the Exchange Fund Ordinance (Cap. 66); and

         (ii)   where such disclosure will enable or assist such person to assist the Monetary Authority in the performance of any of the functions referred to in that section;

(h)   subject to subsection (5D), to the disclosure of information by the Monetary Authority with the consent of-

         (i)   the person from whom the information was obtained or received; and

         (ii)   where the information does not relate to such person, the person to whom it relates; or

(i)   to the disclosure of information which has been made available to the public by virtue of being disclosed in any circumstances

in which, or for any purpose for which, disclosure is not precluded by this section or section 121.

(5A) For the purposes of subsection (5)(f), "authorized statutory office" means-

    (a)   the Insurance Authority under the Insurance Companies Ordinance(Cap.41);or

    (b)   the Securities and Futures Commission.

    (c)-(d) (Repealed)

(5B) The Legislative Council may, by resolution, amend subsection (5A).

(5C) The Monetary Authority may attach a condition to any disclosure of information made pursuant to subsection (5)(b), (c), (d), (e), (1) or (ga), and shall attach a condition to any disclosure of information made pursuant to subsection (5)(g), that neither-

    (a)   the person to whom the information has been disclosed; nor

    (b)   any person obtaining or receiving the information (whether directly or indirectly) from the person referred to in paragraph (a),

shall disclose that information to any other person without the consent of the Monetary Authority.

(5D) Subsection (5)(h) shall not operate to require the Monetary Authority to disclose in or in relation to any civil proceedings any information which he may disclose, or has disclosed, pursuant to that subsection.

(6) Any person who-

    (a)   contravenes subsection (1);

    (b)   aids, abets, counsels or procures any person to contravene subsection (1); or

    (c)   knowing that the condition referred to in subsection (5C) has been attached to a disclosure of information made pursuant to

             subsection (5), contravenes, or aids, abets, counsels or procures any person to contravene, that condition,

commits an offence and is liable-

    (i)   on conviction upon indictment to a fine of $500,000 and to imprisonment for 2 years; or

    (ii)   on summary conviction to a fine of $50,000 and to imprisonment for 6 months.

Disclosure of information relating to authorized institutions

121.(1) Subject to subsection (3), and notwithstanding section 120, theMonetary Authority may disclose information to an authority in a place outside Hong Kong where-

    (a)   that authority exercises functions in that place corresponding to the functions of-

    (i)   the Monetary Authority; or

    (ii)   an authorized statutory office within the meaning of section 120(5A); and

    (b)   in the opinion of the Monetary Authority-

    (i)   that authority is subject to adequate secrecy provisions in that place; and

    (ii)   it is desirable or expedient that information should be so disclosed in the interests of depositors or potential depositors or the public interest; or

    (iii)   such disclosure will enable or assist the recipient of the information to exercise his functions and it is not contrary to the interests of depositors or potential depositors or the public interest that the information should be so disclosed.

(2) Subject to subsection (3) and notwithstanding section 120, the Monetary Authority may, if he considers that it is in the interests of customers of the representative office, provide to the appropriate recognized banking supervisory authority of a place outside Hong Kong which is, in his opinion, subject to adequate secrecy provisions in that place information on matters relating to the affairs of a local representative office which is maintained by a bank incorporated in that place or in respect of which the Monetary Authority is of the opinion that the authority has primary supervisory responsibility.

(2A)   *(Replaced)*

(3)   Under no circumstances shall the Monetary Authority provide any information under this section relating to the affairs of any individual customer of an authorized institution or a local representative office.

Winding-up of authorized institutions

122.(1) The provisions of the Companies Ordinance (Cap. 32) with regard to a creditors' voluntary winding-up shall not apply to authorized institutions.

(2) On a petition by the Financial Secretary, acting in accordance with a direction of the Governor in Council under section 53(1)(iii), the High Court may-

  (a) on any ground specified in section 177 of the Companies Ordinance (Cap. 32); or

  (b) if it is satisfied that it is in the public interest that the authorized institution or former authorized institution should be wound up,

order the winding-up of an authorized institution or former authorized institution in accordance with the provisions of the Companies Ordinance (Cap. 32) relating to the winding-up of companies.

(3) Where before the presentation of a petition for the winding up of an authorized institution by the High Court, and whether or not the petition is presented by the Financial Secretary, there has in respect of the institution been a direction given under section 52(1)(C) which has continued in force at all times until the presentation of the petition, and a winding-up order is made thereon, then, notwithstanding the provisions of section 184(2) of the Companies Ordinance (Cap. 32), the winding up of the institution by the High Court shall, for the purposes of sections 170, 179, 182, 183, 266, 267, 269 and 274, and paragraphs (d), (e), (h), (i), (j), (k), (1) and (o) of section 271(1), of that Ordinance, be deemed to have commenced at the time the direction was so given.

(4) Nothing in section 182 of the Companies Ordinance (Cap. 32) shall invalidate any disposition of the business or property of an authorized institution made by the Manager of the institution, or by the institution under the direction of the Manager, acting in good faith in the course of managing the affairs, business and property of the institution.

(5) Where the Financial Secretary is entitled to petition the High Court by virtue of section 117(5)(f), the High Court may wind up a deposit-taking company or restricted licence bank or former deposit-taking company or restricted licence bank in accordance with the provisions of the Companies Ordinance (Cap. 32) relating to the winding-up of companies if-

  (a) the deposit-taking company or restricted licence bank is unable to pay sums due and payable to its depositors or is able to pay such sums only by defaulting on its obligations; or

  (b) the value of the deposit-taking company's or restricted licence bank's assets is less than the amount of its liabilities.

(6)   Nothing in this section shall authorize the winding-up of a former deposit-taking company or restricted licence bank which does not continue to have any liability in respect of any deposit for which it had a liability at the time when it was authorized.

Offences by directors, managers, trustees, employees and agents

123.   Any director, manager, trustee, employee or agent of any authorized institution who, with intent to deceive-

> *(a)*   wilfully makes, or causes to be made, a false entry in any book of record or in any report, slip, document or statement of the business, affairs, transactions, condition, assets or accounts of the institution;

> *(b)*   wilfully omits to make an entry in any book of record or in any report, slip, document or statement of the business, affairs, transactions, condition, assets or accounts of the institution, or wilfully causes any such entry to be omitted; or

> *(c)*   wilfully alters, abstracts, conceals or destroys an entry in any book of record, or in any report, slip, document or statement of the business, affairs, transactions, condition, assets or accounts of the institution, or wilfully causes any such entry to be altered, abstracted, concealed or destroyed,

commits an offence and is liable-

> **(i)**   on conviction upon indictment to a fine of $500,000 and to imprisonment for 5 years; or

> **(ii)**   on summary conviction to a fine of $50,000 and to imprisonment for 2 years.

Prohibition on receipt of commission by staff

124.   Any director or employee of an authorized institution, who asks for or receives, consents or agrees to receive any gift, commission, emolument, service, gratuity, money, property or thing of value for his own personal benefit or advantage or for that of any of his relatives, for procuring or endeavouring to procure for any person any advance, loan, financial guarantee or credit facility from that institution or the purchase or discount of any draft, note, cheque, bill of exchange or other obligation by that institution, or for permitting any person to overdraw any account with that institution, commits an offence and is liable-

> *(a)*   on conviction upon indictment to a fine of $100,000 and to imprisonment for 5 years; or

    (b)   on summary conviction to a fine of $50,000 and to imprisonment for 2 years.

Search warrants and seizures

125.(1) If a magistrate is satisfied by information on oath that there is reasonable ground for suspecting that an offence under this Ordinance has been committed, the magistrate may issue a warrant empowering any police officer to enter and search any premises specified in the warrant.

(2) A police officer to whom a warrant is issued under subsection (1)

may-

    (a)   break open any outer or inner door of or in any premises which he is empowered by the warrant to enter and search;

    (b)   inspect, seize and remove anything which the police officer has reasonable grounds for believing to be or to contain evidence of an offence under this Ordinance; and

    (c)   remove by force any person who obstructs any entry, search, inspection, seizure or removal which he is empowered by this subsection to make.

(3) A person from whom any books, accounts or other documents have been seized and removed under subsection (2) shall, pending any proceedings for an offence under this Ordinance, be entitled to take copies of or extracts from such books, accounts or other documents.

(4) Any person who obstructs a police officer in the exercise of any power conferred on him by subsection (2) commits an offence and is liable on conviction upon indictment or on summary conviction to a fine of $50,000 and to imprisonment for 6 months.

Defence where director or manager, etc. prosecuted

126.(1) Subject to subsection (2), in proceedings for an offence under this Ordinance it shall be a defence for the person charged to prove that he took all reasonable precautions and exercised all due diligence to avoid the commission of such an offence by himself or any person under his control.

(2)   Subsection (1) shall not apply to an offence under section 46(8), 47(2) or (3), 50(6), 64(5), 72A(4), 73(2), 97(1), 117(7), 118(5), 120, 123 or 124.

Limit of time for complaint or information

126A.(1) In any case of an offence other than an indictable offence the complaint shall be made to or information laid before a magistrate, or an officer of a magistrate's court who is authorized in writing for that purpose by a magistrate, at any time within 3 years after the commission of the offence and within 6 months after evidence sufficient in the opinion of the Attorney General to justify prosecution comes to his knowledge.

(2) For the purposes of subsection (1) a certificate of the Attorney General as to the date on which such evidence as is mentioned in subsection (1) came to his knowledge shall be conclusive evidence of that fact.

Indemnity

127.(1) No liability shall be incurred by-

    (a)   any public officer;

    (b)   any person appointed under section 5A(3) of the Exchange Fund Ordinance (Cap. 66) to assist the Monetary Authority;

    (c)   the Advisor of an authorized institution or any person appointed under section 53 G (5) by the Advisor;

    (d)   the Manager of an authorized institution or any person appointed under section 53G(5) by the Manager; or

    (e)   any person appointed under section 117(2),

as a result of anything done or omitted to be done by him bona fide in the exercise or purported exercise of any functions conferred or imposed by or under this Ordinance.

(2) No liability shall be incurred by any chief executive, director, manager or employee of an authorized institution as a result of anything done or omitted to be done by him in good faith in the carrying out or purported carrying out of any directions given to him by the Manager of the institution.

128.   *(Repealed)*

Validity of contract in contravention of this Ordinance or

any Ordinance repealed by this Ordinance

129.(1) Subject to section 70B(4) and (5), the contravention of any prohibition in this Ordinance or in any Ordinance repealed by this Ordinance on the entering into of any contract shall not render that contract unenforceable.

(2) Subsection (1) shall be deemed to have had effect from 1 April 1976, so, however, that nothing in that subsection as read with this subsection shall have effect in relation to any legal proceedings commenced before the commencement of this Ordinance.

(3) Subject to section 70B(4) and (5), for the avoidance of doubt, it is hereby declared that the contravention of any prohibition in this Ordinance or in any Ordinance repealed by this Ordinance on the entering into of any contract shall not render that contract void.

(4) In this section, "contract" includes a deed which is not otherwise a contract.

(5) This section shall not operate to prejudice the operation of section 53B(5) or (8), 53C(7) or (8) or 53E(1)(ii).

130.   *(Repealed)*

Recovery of fees, expenses, etc.

131.(1) There shall be recoverable at the suit of the Attorney General as a civil debt due to the Crown from the authorized institution concerned

　　　　(a)　　the amount of any fees payable under section 19, 45, 48 or 51;

　　　　(b)　　any remuneration and expenses payable by the authorized institution pursuant to a determination under section 53G(7) to-

　　　　　　　　(i)　　the Advisor of the institution or any person appointed under section 53G(5) by the Advisor;

　　　　　　　　(ii)　　the Manager of the institution or any person appointed under section 53G(5) by the Manager;

　　　　(c)　　*(Repealed)*

　　　　(d)　　any expenses ordered by the Financial Secretary to be defrayed by the authorized institution under section 55(3).

　　　　(e)　　*(Repealed)*

(2) There shall be recoverable, at the suit of the Attorney General, as a civil debt due from the applicants, jointly and severally, to the Crown, any expenses ordered by the Financial Secretary to be defrayed by the applicants under section 55(3).

(3) Subject to subsection (5), any sum recoverable under this section at the suit of the Attorney General shall be a debt due to the Crown within the meaning of section 265(1)(d) of the Companies Ordinance (Cap. 32) and section 38(1)(d) of the Bankruptcy Ordinance (Cap. 6).

(4) The fees, remuneration, expenses and sums of money recoverable under this section shall be paid to the Director of Accounting Services.

(5) Any remuneration and expenses referred to in subsection (1)(b) payable by an authorized institution shall, in any winding up by the High Court of the institution, have the same priority as is given under rule 179(1) of the Companies (Winding-up) Rules (Cap. 32 sub. leg.) to any costs, charges and expenses incurred by the Official Receiver.

Cost related fees to be paid into Exchange Fund

131A. Any part of monies paid to the Director of Accounting Services under section 19, 45, 48, 51 or 131(4), which relates to the administrative or other costs incurred or likely to be incurred by the Exchange Fund in connection with or otherwise in relation to the performance of any function under this Ordinance, shall be paid by him into the Exchange Fund.

Use of language

132.(1) All entries in books and accounts kept by authorized institutions shall be recorded in the Chinese or English language and the Arabic system of numerals shall be employed.

(2) All forms and information required to be sent and all returns required to be made to the Monetary Authority pursuant to any of the provisions of this Ordinance shall be compiled in the Chinese or English language and the Arabic system of numerals and, if any such form, information or return is a translation, be certified to the satisfaction of the Monetary Authority as a true and correct translation.

(3) Every director and every manager of an authorized institution which contravenes subsection (1) or (2) commits an offence and is liable on conviction upon indictment or on summary conviction to a fine of $50,000 and, in the case of a continuing offence, to a further fine of $5,000 for every day during which the offence continues.

Power of Monetary Authority to specify forms

133.(1) Subject to subsection (2), the Monetary Authority may specify the form of any document required under this Ordinance to be in the specified form and the form of such other documents required for the purposes of this Ordinance as he thinks fit.

(2) The Monetary Authority's power under subsection (1), shall be subject to any express requirement under this Ordinance for a form, whether specified or otherwise, to comply with that requirement, but that requirement shall not restrict the exercise of that power in respect of that form to the extent that, in the opinion of the Monetary Authority, his exercise of that power in respect of that form does not contravene that requirement.

(3) For the avoidance of doubt, it is hereby declared that the Monetary Authority's power under subsection (1) may be exercised in such a way as to-

> (a) include in the specified form of any document referred to in that subsection a statutory declaration-

(i)   to be made by the person completing the form; and

(ii)   as to whether the particulars contained in the form are true and correct to the best of that person's knowledge and belief;

(b)   specify 2 or more forms of any document referred to in that subsection, whether as alternatives, or to provide for particular circumstances or particular cases, as the Monetary Authority thinks fit.

(4)   A form specified under this section shall be-

(a)   completed in accordance with such directions and instructions as are specified in the form;

(b)   accompanied by such documents as are specified in the form; and

(c)   if the completed form is required to be provided to the Monetary Authority or any other person, so provided in the manner, if any, specified in the form.

(5)   In this section, "document" includes any accounts, application, notice and certificate.

Service of notices

134.(1) Subject to subsection (2), a notice (howsoever described) which is required to be served under this Ordinance, or which may be served under this Ordinance, on an authorized institution shall, in the absence of evidence to the contrary, be deemed to be so served if it is-

(a)   left at;

(b)   sent by post to; or

(c)   sent by telex, facsimile transmission or other similar method to, the institution's principal place of business in Hong Kong.

(2) A variation, notice, resolution or determination referred to in section 52(2)(b)(i) , 53A(2)(b)(i), 53B(7)(b) or (8), 53F(3)(b)(i) or 53G(3)(b) or (8)(b)(iii) which under that section is required to be, or may be, served on an authorized institution incorporated outside Hong Kong at its principal place of business outside Hong Kong shall, in the absence of evidence to the contrary, be deemed to be so served if it is-

(a)   given to or served on an officer, within the meaning of section 2(1) of the Companies Ordinance (Cap. 32), of the institution at that place;

(b)   sent by post to that place; or

(c)   sent by telex, facsimile transmission or other similar method to that place.

(3) Subsection (1) shall not operate to limit the generality of section 356 of the Companies Ordinance (Cap. 32).

(4) Notwithstanding any other provision of this Ordinance (including any such provision referred to in subsection (2)), subsection (2) shall not operate to limit the generality of section 333 of the Companies Ordinance (Cap. 32) and, accordingly, a variation, notice, resolution or determination referred to in that subsection may be served on a person resident in Hong Kong who has been authorized as specified in subsection (1)(c) of that section by the authorized institution concerned.

Monetary Authority to consult, etc., before attaching conditions to authorization

134A.(1) Before exercising any power under section 16 to attach to the authorization of any authorized institution any condition (including attach by way of amending conditions already attached to the authorization), the Monetary Authority shall, where he proposes to attach that condition to the authorization of-

(a)   each authorized institution, consult with the following persons-

(i)   the Banking Advisory Committee;

(ii)   the Deposit-taking Companies Advisory Committee;

(iii)   The Hong Kong Association of Banks incorporated by section 3 of The Hong Kong Association of Banks Ordinance (Cap. 364); and

(iv)   The DTC Association (The Hong Kong Association of Restricted Licence Banks and Deposit-Taking Companies) incorporated under the Companies Ordinance (Cap. 32) (including any successor thereof);

(b)   each authorized institution which is a bank, or which belongs to a class of banks, consult with the persons referred to in paragraph (a)(i) and (iii) or with each such institution;

> *(c)* each authorized institution which is a deposit-taking company or restricted licence bank, or which belongs to a class of deposit-taking companies or restricted licence banks, consult with the persons referred to in paragraph (a)(ii) and (iv) or with each such institution;
>
> *(d)* a particular authorized institution, give that institution an opportunity, within such period as the Monetary Authority may specify in writing, being a period reasonable in all the circumstances, of being heard.

(2) For the avoidance of doubt, it is hereby declared that any requirement under subsection (1) for the Monetary Authority to consult with persons referred to in that subsection in respect of any matter referred to in that subsection shall not operate to prevent the Monetary Authority from consulting with such other persons as he thinks fit in respect of that matter.

Power to amend Schedules

135.(1) The Governor in Council may, by notice in the Gazette, amend the First, Seventh or Eighth Schedule.

(2) The Legislative Council may, by resolution, amend the Second Schedule.

(3) The Financial Secretary may, by notice in the Gazette, amend the Third, Fourth, Fifth, Ninth or Tenth Schedule.

(4) *(Repealed)*

Consent of Attorney General

136. No prosecution in respect of any offence under this Ordinance shall be instituted without the consent in writing of the Attorney General.

137. *(Amendments Incorporated)*

Exclusion of provisions of Gambling Ordinance

137A.(1) Subject to subsection (2), the Gambling Ordinance (Cap. 148) shall not apply to any transaction proposed to be entered into, or entered into, by an authorized institution.

(2) Subsection (1) shall not apply to a transaction, or a transaction belonging to a class of transactions, specified by the Monetary Authority by notice in the Gazette as being a transaction, or a class of transactions, as the case may be, to which that subsection shall not apply.

Prescribed instruments

137B.(1)   In this Ordinance-

"prescribed instrument"-

    (a)   means an instrument-

        (i)   specified in the Sixth Schedule; and

        (ii)   in respect of which the Monetary Authority, or a person approved under subsection (3)(a) for the purposes of this definition, is the bearer for the purposes of facilitating services for the clearing and settlement of transactions in that instrument; and

    (b)   includes any right or interest-

        (i)   arising, whether directly or indirectly, under, or in respect of, an instrument referred to in paragraph (a), and irrespective of whether the right or interest may be enforced, claimed or otherwise maintained-

            (A)   by a person against the issuer of the instrument; or

            (B)   by another person against the person referred to in sub-subparagraph (A); and

        (ii)   which may be evidenced by-

            (A)   a written document;

            (B)   information recorded in the form of any entry in a book of account;

            (C)   information recorded (whether by means of a computer or otherwise) in a non-legible form but which is capable of being reproduced in a legible form; or

            (D)   any combination of sub-subparagraphs (A), (B) and (C).

(2) Where, but for this subsection, a prescribed instrument would be a security within the meaning of the Securities Ordinance (Cap. 333), then, notwithstanding the provisions of that Ordinance, the prescribed instrument shall be deemed not to be such a security if, and only if, the instrument concerned specified in the Sixth Schedule is not such a security.

(3) The Monetary Authority may, by notice in the Gazette-

> *(a)* approve a person for the purposes of the definition of "prescribed instrument";
>
> *(b)* amend the Sixth Schedule.

(4) For the avoidance of doubt, it is hereby declared that a notice under subsection (3)(a) is not subsidiary legislation.

PART XXII - Transitional, Savings And Repeal

Interpretation

138. In this Part, unless the context otherwise requires-

"former bank" means a bank which, immediately before the commencement of this Ordinance, held a former banking licence;

"former Banking Advisory Committee" means the Banking Advisory Committee established by section 3 of the former Banking Ordinance and as constituted immediately before the commencement of this Ordinance;

"former banking licence" means a licence granted under section 7 or 42 of the former Banking Ordinance and in force immediately before the commencement of this Ordinance;

"former Banking Ordinance (Cap. 155, 1983 Ed.)" means the Banking Ordinance 1964 repealed by this Ordinance;

"former Commissioner" means the person who was, immediately before the commencement of this Ordinance, the Commissioner of Banking under section 4 of the former Banking Ordinance and, for the purposes of this

Part, any reference in the former Deposit-taking Companies Ordinance to the Commissioner of Deposit-taking Companies shall be deemed to be a reference to such Commissioner of Banking;

"former Deposit-taking Companies Advisory Committee" means the Deposit-taking Companies Advisory Committee established by section 4 ofthe former Deposit-taking Companies Ordinance and as constituted immediately before the commencement of this Ordinance;

"former Deposit-taking Companies Ordinance (Cap. 328, 1983 Ed.)" means the Deposit-taking Companies Ordinance 1976 repealed by this Ordinance;

"former deposit-taking licence" means a licence granted under section 16B of the former Deposit-taking Companies Ordinance and in force immediately before the commencement of this Ordinance;

"former registration" means registration under section 10 of the former Deposit-taking Companies Ordinance which was in force immediately before the commencement of this Ordinance.

Banking Ordinance

Appointed members of former committees to continue in office

139.(1) Any member of the former Banking Advisory Committee who was such a member by virtue of an appointment under section 3(2) of the former Banking Ordinance shall, on and from the commencement of this Ordinance, be deemed to be a member of the Banking Advisory Committee as if, on that commencement, he had been appointed under section 4(2) to be a member of the Banking Advisory Committee for the period he had left to serve, immediately before that commencement, as a member of the former Banking Advisory Committee and, for that purpose and for that period, the terms on which he was so appointed as a member of the former Banking Advisory Committee shall be the terms on which he shall be a member of the Banking Advisory Committee.

(2) Any member of the former Deposit-taking Companies Advisory Committee who was such a member by virtue of an appointment under section 5(1)(c) of the former Deposit-taking Companies Ordinance shall, on and from the commencement of this Ordinance, be deemed to be a member of the Deposit-taking Companies Advisory Committee as if, on that commencement, he had been appointed under section 5(2) to be a member of the Deposit-taking Companies Advisory Committee for the period he had left to serve, immediately before that commencement, as a member of the former Deposit-taking Companies Advisory Committee and, for that purpose and for that period, the terms on which he was so appointed as a member of the former Deposit-taking Companies Advisory Committee shall be the terms on which he shall be a member of the Deposit-taking Companies Advisory Committee.

140. *(Repealed)*

Authorized and employed persons to continue to be

authorized and employed

141. Any person who was, immediately before the commencement of this Ordinance, authorized or employed under section 4A of the former Banking Ordinance to assist the former Commissioner in the exercise of his functions and duties under the former Banking Ordinance, either generally or in any particular case, shall, on and from the commencement of this Ordinance, be deemed, in the like capacity, to be authorized or employed to assist the Commissioner in the exercise of his functions under this Ordinance as if, on that commencement, he had been, in the like capacity, authorized or employed under section 8 to assist the Commissioner in the exercise of his functions under this Ordinance for the period he had left, immediately before that commencement, to be so authorized or employed under the former Banking Ordinance.

Former applications for licenses, etc. deemed to be applications

under this Ordinance

142. Where, immediately before the commencement of this Ordinance, there was in existence-

    (a)   an application for a former banking licence under section 6 of

the former Banking Ordinance in relation to which the Governor in Council had not granted or refused a former banking licence under section 7 of the former Banking Ordinance;

(b)   an application for former registration under section 9 of the former Deposit-taking Companies Ordinance in relation to which there has not been any registration or refusal of registration by the Commissioner under section 10 of the former Deposit-taking Companies Ordinance; or

(c)   an application for a former deposit-taking licence under section 16A of the former Deposit-taking Companies Ordinance in relation to which the Financial Secretary had not granted or refused a former deposit-taking licence under section 16B of the former Deposit-taking Companies Ordinance,

then-

(i)   in the case of an application referred to in paragraph (a), the application shall be deemed to be an application under section 15 for a banking licence;

(ii)   in the case of an application referred to in paragraph (b), the application shall be deemed to be an application under section 20 for registration; and

(iii)   in the case of an application referred to in paragraph (c), the application shall be deemed to be an application under section 24 for a deposit-taking license,

and the provisions of this Ordinance shall apply accordingly.

Former licences, etc. deemed to be licences, etc. under this Ordinance

143.(1) Any former banking licence shall, on and from the commencement of this Ordinance, be deemed to be-

(a)   in the case of a former banking licence granted under section 7 of the former Banking Ordinance, a banking licence granted under section 16;

(b)   (Repealed)

and the provisions of this Ordinance shall apply accordingly.

(2) Any former registration shall, on and from the commencement of this Ordinance, be deemed to be registration under section 21, and the provisions of this Ordinance shall apply accordingly.

(3) Any former deposit-taking licence shall, on and from the commencement of this Ordinance, be deemed to be a deposit-taking licence granted under section 25, and the provisions of this Ordinance shall apply accordingly.

(4) Notwithstanding Part VII of the former Deposit-taking Companies Ordinance, any former registration or former deposit-taking licence which was, immediately before the commencement of this Ordinance, suspended under that Part shall, on and from that commencement, but subject to section 146, be deemed, for the purposes of subsections (2) and (3) and the definitions of "former registration" and "former deposit-taking licence" in section 138, to be in force immediately before that commencement.

Date of payment of certain fees

144. Where, under this Ordinance, a bank, registered deposit-taking company or licensed deposit-taking company is required to pay any fee specified in the Second Schedule, irrespective of whether the words "authorized institution" are used to create any such requirement, by reference to the anniversary of the date on which the bank, registered deposit-taking company or licensed deposit-taking company was licensed or registered, as the case may be, or words to that effect, and the banking licence, registration or deposit-taking licence, as the case may be, held by that bank, registered deposit-taking company or licensed deposit-taking company is deemed by virtue of section 143 to be a banking licence, registration or deposit-taking licence, as the case may be, then, for the purposes of paying any such fee, and notwithstanding any other provision of this Ordinance, such reference to the anniversary of the date on which the bank, registered deposit-taking company or licensed deposit-taking company was incensed or registered shall be the anniversary of the date on which the bank, registered deposit-taking company or licensed deposit-taking company was licensed or registered, as the case may be, under the former Banking Ordinance or former Deposit-taking Companies Ordinance, as the case may be.

Conditions attached to former licences, etc. deemed to be

conditions under this Ordinance

145.(1) Where, immediately before the commencement of this Ordinance, there was in force any condition attached to a former banking licence under section 7(1)(b) or 7A of the former Banking Ordinance and, on and from that commencement, the former banking licence is deemed by virtue of section 143 to be a banking licence, then, on and from that commencement, any such condition shall be deemed to be a condition attached to the banking licence as if, on that commencement, the Governor in Council had attached such condition under section 17 to the banking licence, and the provisions of this Ordinance shall apply accordingly.

(2) Where, immediately before the commencement of this Ordinance, there was in force any condition attached to a former deposit-taking licence under section 16B(1)(a) or (3) of the former Deposit-taking Companies Ordinance and, on and from that commencement, the former deposit-taking licence is deemed by virtue of section 143 to be a deposit-taking licence, then, on and from that commencement, any such condition shall be deemed to be a condition attached to the deposit-taking licence as if, on that commencement, the Financial Secretary had attached such condition under section 25(3) to the deposit-taking licence, and the provisions of this Ordinance shall apply accordingly.

(3) Where any local branch to which section 44(3) applies had in force, immediately before the commencement of this Ordinance, an approval under section 12A(1) or (3) of the former Banking Ordinance or section 16H(1) or (3) of the former Deposit-taking Companies Ordinance to which was attached any condition under section 12A(4) of the former Banking Ordinance or section 16H(4) of the former Deposit-taking Companies Ordinance and which condition was in force immediately before that commencement, then, on and from that commencement, any such condition shall be deemed to be attached to the approval under section 44 of the local branch as if, on that commencement, the Commissioner had attached such condition under section 44(4) to the approval, and the provisions of this Ordinance shall apply accordingly.

(4) Where any local representative office to which section 46(2) applies had in force, immediately before the commencement of this Ordinance, an approval under section 12C(1) or (2) of the former Banking Ordinance to which was attached any condition under section 12C(4) of the former Banking Ordinance and which condition was in force immediately before that commencement, then, on and from that commencement, any such condition shall be deemed to be attached to the approval under section 46 of the local representative office as if, on that commencement, the Commissioner had attached such condition under section 46(4) to the approval, and the provisions of this Ordinance shall apply accordingly.

(5) Where any overseas branch or overseas representative office to which section 49(3) applies had in force, immediately before the commencement of this Ordinance, an approval under section 12 F(1) or (3) of the former Banking Ordinance or section 16J(1) or (3) of the former Deposit-taking Companies Ordinance to which was attached any condition under section 12F(4) of the former Banking Ordinance or section 16J(4) of the former Deposit-taking Companies Ordinance and which condition was in force immediately before that commencement, then, on and from that commencement, any such condition shall be deemed to be attached to the approval under section 49 of the overseas branch or overseas representative office, as the case may be, as if, on that commencement, the Commissioner had attached such condition under section 49(4) to the approval, and the provisions of this Ordinance shall apply accordingly.

Suspension of former registration, etc. deemed to be suspension

under this Ordinance

146. Where any former registration or former deposit-taking licence which is, on and from the commencement of this Ordinance, deemed by virtue of section 143 to be registration or a deposit-taking licence, was, immediately before that commencement, suspended under Part VII of the former Deposit-taking Companies Ordinance, then, on and from that commencement, that registration or

that deposit-taking licence, as the case may be, shall, in the like manner, be deemed to be suspended under Part VI for the period concerned of such suspension left to serve immediately before that commencement as if, on that commencement and for that period, the designated authority under Part VI had suspended that registration or deposit-taking licence, as the case may be, and the provisions of this Ordinance shall apply accordingly.

Actions, etc. under Part IV of former Banking Ordinance deemed to be

actions under Part X of this Ordinance

147. Where an act, matter or thing has been done under Part IV of the former Banking Ordinance by the Commissioner, the Financial Secretary or the Governor in Council to or in relation to a former bank and, on and from the commencement of this Ordinance, the former banking licence held by the former bank is deemed by virtue of section 143 to be a banking licence, then, on and from that commencement, to the extent that but for the enactment of this Ordinance that act, matter or thing would on or after that commencement have had any force or effect or been in operation, that act, matter or thing shall, in the like manner, be deemed to have been done under Part X by the Commissioner, the Financial Secretary or the Governor in Council, as the case may be, to or in relation to the bank which holds that banking licence as if, on that commencement, that act, matter or thing were, to that extent, done under Part X by the Commissioner, the Financial Secretary or the Governor in Council, as the case may be, to or in relation to the bank, and the provisions of this Ordinance shall apply accordingly.

Transitional provision in relation to certain letters of comfort

148. A letter of comfort which was, immediately before the day of commencement of the Banking (Amendment) (No. 2) Ordinance 1991, deemed by section 148 at all mes to have been accepted under paragraph (c) of the proviso to section 81(2) shall, on and from that date, be deemed at all times to have been accepted under section 81(6)(b), and the provisions of this Ordinance shall apply accordingly.

Transitional provisions in relation to section 87

148A.(1) Where, immediately before 1 September 1986, any period allowed under the proviso to section 27(1) of the former Banking Ordinance, or under section 23B(3) of the former Deposit-taking Companies Ordinance, had not expired then, on and from that date, the unexpired portion of that period shall be deemed to be a further period approved under, and for the purposes of, the proviso to section 87(1) as if, on that date, the Commissioner had given such approval under the proviso to section 87(1), and the provisions of this Ordinance shall apply accordingly.

(2) Where, immediately before 1 September 1986, any period allowed under section 23B(2) of the former Deposit-taking Companies Ordinance had not expired then, on and from that date, the unexpired portion of that period shall be deemed to be a further period approved under, and for the purposes of, section 87(2)(a) as if, on that date, the Commissioner had given such approval under section 87(2)(a), and the provisions of this Ordinance shall apply accordingly.

(3) Where, immediately before 1 September 1986, there was in force any approval under section 27(2) of the former Banking Ordinance then, on and from that date, any such approval shall be deemed to be an approval under, and for the purposes of, section 87(2)(b) as if, on that date, the Commissioner had given such approval under section 87(2)(b).

Transitional provisions in relation to amendments made by Banking

(Amendment) Ordinance 1990

149.(1) In this section-

"deposit-taking licence" means a deposit-taking licence-

(a)   granted, or deemed to be granted, under section 25 as in force at any time before the relevant day; and

(b)   in force immediately before the relevant day;

"licensed deposit-taking company" means a company which, immediately before the relevant day, held a deposit-taking licence;

"relevant day" means the day of commencement of the relevant Ordinance;

"relevant Ordinance" means the Banking (Amendment) Ordinance 1990.

(2) Where, immediately before the relevant day, there was an application for a deposit-taking licence under section 24 in relation to which the Financial Secretary had not granted or refused a deposit-taking licence under section 25 then, on and from the relevant day, that application shall be deemed to be an application under section 24 for a restricted banking licence, and the provisions of this Ordinance shall apply accordingly.

(3) Any deposit-taking licence shall, on and from the relevant day, be deemed to be a restricted banking licence granted under section 25, and the provisions of this Ordinance shall apply accordingly.

(4) Notwithstanding Part VI as in force immediately before the relevant day, any deposit-taking licence which was, immediately before the relevant day, suspended under that Part shall, on and from the relevant day, be deemed, for the purposes of subsection (3) and the definition of "deposit-taking licence" in subsection (1), to have been in force immediately before the relevant day.

(5) Where, immediately before the relevant day, there was in force any

condition attached or deemed to be attached to a deposit-taking licence under section 25 and, on and from the relevant day, the deposit-taking licence is deemed by virtue of subsection (3) to be a restricted banking licence, then, on and from the relevant day, any such condition shall be deemed to be a condition attached to the restricted banking licence as if, on the relevant day, the Financial

Secretary had attached such condition under section 25 to the restricted banking licence, and the provisions of this Ordinance shall apply accordingly.

(6) Where any deposit-taking licence which is, on and from the relevant day, deemed by virtue of subsection (3) to be a restricted banking licence, was, immediately before the relevant day, suspended under Part VI, then, on and from the relevant day, that restricted banking licence shall, in the like manner, be deemed to be suspended under Part VI for the period concerned of such suspension left to serve immediately before the relevant day as if, on the relevant day and for that period, the designated authority under Part VI had suspended that restricted anking licence, and the provisions of this Ordinance shall apply accordingly.

(7) Where an act, matter or thing has been done or deemed to be done under Part X as in force at any time before the relevant day by the Commissioner, the Financial Secretary or the Governor in Council to or in relation to a licensed deposit-taking company and, on and from the relevant day, the deposit-taking licence held by that company is deemed by virtue of subsection (3) to be a restricted banking licence, then, on and from the relevant day, to the extent that but for the enactment of the relevant Ordinance that act, matter or thing would on or after the relevant day have had any force or effect or been in operation, that act, matter or thing shall, in the like manner, be deemed to have been done under Part X by the Commissioner, the Financial Secretary or the Governor in Council, as the case may be, to or in relation to the restricted licence bank which holds that restricted banking licence as if, on the relevant day, that act, matter or thing were, to that extent, done under Part X by the Commissioner, the Financial Secretary or the Governor in Council, as the case may be, to or in relation to the restricted licence bank, and the provisions of this Ordinance shall apply accordingly.

(8) To the extent that any of the other provisions of this Part have any force or effect or are in operation on or after the relevant day, any reference in those provisions to-

> *(a)* a deposit-taking licence shall be deemed to be a reference to a restricted banking licence; and
>
> *(b)* a licensed deposit-taking company shall be deemed to be a reference to a restricted licence bank,

and the provisions of this Ordinance shall apply accordingly.

(9)-(13) *(Repealed)*

Transitional provisions in relation to amendments made by Banking

(Amendment)(No. 2) Ordinance 1991

150.(1) In this section-

> "relevant day" means the day of commencement of the relevant Ordinance;
>
> "relevant Ordinance" means the Banking (Amendment) (No. 2) Ordinance 1991.

(2) Section 70 shall not apply to a person becoming a controller of an authorized institution on or from the relevant day where the acts or circumstances by virtue of which he became such a controller substantially occurred before the relevant day.

(3) The definition of "controller" in section 2(1), and sections 70, 72, 72A and 126, as in force immediately before the relevant day, shall, on and from the relevant day, apply to a person referred to in subsection (2) as they would have applied to that person if the relevant Ordinance had never been enacted.

(4) Where, immediately before the relevant day, there was in existence an application for an approval under section 70 or 72 in relation to which the Commissioner had not granted, or refused to grant, such approval, then, at any time on and from the relevant day, the Commissioner may grant, or refuse to grant, such approval as if the relevant Ordinance had never been enacted, and any such grant of, or refusal to grant, such approval made on or after the relevant day shall have such force or effect or operation as such grant of, or refusal to grant, such approval would have had if the relevant Ordinance had never been enacted.

(5) Where any person to whom section 70 or 72, as in force immediately before the relevant day, applied to had not, before the relevant day, made an application under that section for an approval in respect of the matter by virtue of which that section applies to him, then, on and from the relevant day, that section shall apply to him in respect of such matter as if the relevant Ordinance had never been enacted.

(6) Where, immediately before the relevant day, there was in existence an approval (including any conditions to which such approval is subject), or refusal to grant an approval, under section 70 or 72, then, on and from the relevant day, any such approval (including any conditions to which such approval is subject) or refusal shall have such force or effect or operation as such approval or refusal would have continued to have had if the relevant Ordinance had never been enacted.

(7) For the avoidance of doubt, it is hereby declared that where subsection (3), (4), (5) or (6) applies in relation to any person at any time on and from the relevant day, such application shall be without prejudice to the application of the provisions of Part XIII in relation to such person at any time on and from the relevant day.

(8)   Where an authorized institution contravenes section 74(1)-

    (a)   by failing to appoint not less than one alternate chief executive of the institution; and

    (b)   at any time before the expiration of the period of 6 months immediately following the relevant day, or such further period as the Monetary Authority approves for the purposes of the application of section 71 to any person the institution proposes to appoint as an alternate chief executive,

section 74(2) shall not apply in relation to that contravention (including at any time on or after the expiration of that period or further period, as the case may be).

(9) The financial exposure of an authorized institution under section 81(2) shall not include financial exposure for any item referred to in paragraph (c) of that section until a notice under section 81(3) in respect of that item is published in the Gazette.

(10) Where an authorized institution contravenes section 81(1), 83(1) or(2)(a), 87(1), 88(1) or 90(1) at any time before the expiration of the period ofone year immediately following the relevant day, or such further period as the Monetary Authority approves in writing in any particular case-

> *(a)* section 81(9), 83(7), 87(3), 88(6) or 90(3), as the case may be, shall not, subject to paragraph (b), apply in relation to that contravention (including at any time on or after the expiration of that period or further period, as the case may be); and

> *(b)* the institution shall, for so long as that contravention of that section continues, comply with that section as if the words "paid-up capital and reserves" were substituted for the words "capital base" appearing in that section and, accordingly, section 81(9), 83(7), 87(3), 88(6) or 90(3), as the case may be, shall apply in relation to any contravention of that section by that institution as that section applies to that institution with those substituted words.

Savings in relation to Exchange Fund (Amendment) Ordinance 1992

151.(1) Notwithstanding the repeal of section 8 of this Ordinance by section 16 of the relevant Ordinance, where immediately before the commencement of the relevant Ordinance, a person was authorized or employed as a result of an exercise of a power under that repealed section, the exercise of such power shall continue to have effect and be regarded as having been exercised by the Monetary Authority.

(2) The repeal referred to in subsection (1) shall not be construed as affecting any authorization or employment to which section 141 applied immediately before the commencement of the relevant Ordinance.

(3) Where immediately before the commencement of the relevant Ordinance-

> *(a)* there was in existence an application to which section 142 then applied;

> *(b)* there was in force any condition to which section 145(3), (4) or (5) then applied;

(c)   an act, matter or thing to which section 147 then applied had any force or effect or was in operation;

(d)   there was in existence an approval to which section 148A then applied;

(e)   an act, matter or thing to which section 149(7) then applied had any force or effect or was in operation; or

(f)   there was in existence an application to which section 150(4) then applied,

then, on and from the commencement of the relevant Ordinance, the section of this Ordinance which, having regard to paragraph (a), (b), (c), (d), (e) or (f) is the relevant section, shall, in relation to such application, condition, act, matter or thing or approval as may be appropriate, be construed and have effect as if any reference therein to the "Commissioner" were substituted for by a reference to the "Monetary Authority".

(4) Notwithstanding the amendment of section 150(8) and (10) by section25(2) of the relevant Ordinance, any further period granted under section 150(8)or (10) and which on the commencement of the relevant Ordinance had notexpired, shall continue to run as if that section had not been so amended.

(5)   Where-

(a)   any act, matter or thing which the Monetary Authority is required, empowered or authorized to do under or pursuant to any enactment, on or after the commencement of the relevant Ordinance, was done by any person other than the Monetary Authority before such commencement; and

(b)   the act, matter or thing was in force or existence immediately before such commencement,

that act, matter or thing shall continue in force, or where appropriate, to exist, on and from such commencement, as if it had been done by the Monetary Authority.

(6) In this section "relevant Ordinance" means the Exchange Fund (Amendment) Ordinance 1992.

Transitional provisions in relation to Banking (Amendment) Ordinance 1995

152.(1) In this section-

"former banking licence" means a banking licence-

(a)   granted, or deemed to be granted, under section 16 as in force at any time before the relevant day; and *(b)*   in force immediately before the relevant day;

"former registration" means registration-

    (a)   given, or deemed to be given, under section 21 as in force at any time before the relevant day; and

    (b)   in force immediately before the relevant day;

"former restricted banking licence" means a restricted banking licence-

    (a)   granted, or deemed to be granted, under section 25 as in force at any time before the relevant day; and

    (b)   in force immediately before the relevant day;

"relevant day" means the day of commencement of the relevant Ordinance;

"relevant Ordinance" means the Banking (Amendment) Ordinance 1995.

(2) Where, immediately before the relevant day, there was in existence-

    (a)   an application for a banking licence under section 15 in relation to which the Governor in Council has not granted or refused a banking licence under section 16;

    (b)   an application for registration as a deposit-taking company

            under section 20 in relation to which there has not been any registration or refusal of registration by the Monetary Authority under section 21; or

    (c)   an application for a restricted banking licence under section 24 in relation to which the Financial Secretary has not granted or refused a restricted banking licence under section 25,

then, on and from the relevant day, the application shall be deemed to be an application under section 15 for authorization to carry on-

    (i)   in the case of paragraph (a), banking business;

    (ii)   in the case of paragraph (b), a business of taking deposits as a deposit-taking company;

    (iii)   in the case of paragraph (c), a business of taking deposits as a restricted licence bank,

and the provisions of this Ordinance shall apply accordingly.

(3) Any former banking licence, former registration or former restricted banking licence shall, on and from the relevant day, be deemed to be-

> *(a)* in the case of a former banking licence, a banking licence granted under section 16;

> *(b)* in the case of former registration, registration under that section;

> *(c)* in the case of a former restricted banking licence, a restricted banking licence granted under that section,

and the provisions of this Ordinance shall apply accordingly.

(4) Notwithstanding Part VI as in force immediately before the relevant day, any former registration or former restricted banking licence which was, immediately before the relevant day, suspended under that Part shall, on and from the relevant day, be deemed to have been in force immediately before the relevant day for the purposes of-

> *(a)* in the case of former registration, subsection (3) and the definition of "former registration" in subsection (1);

> *(b)* in the case of a former restricted banking licence, subsection (3) and the definition of "former restricted banking licence" in subsection (1).

(5) Where-

> *(a)* immediately before the relevant day, there was in force any condition attached or deemed to be attached to -

>> **(i)** a former banking licence under section 16 or 17;

>> **(ii)** former registration under section 21 or 22; or

>> **(iii)** a former restricted banking licence under section 25; and

> *(b)* on and from the relevant day, that former banking licence, former registration or former restricted banking licence is deemed by virtue of subsection (3) to be a banking licence, registration or restricted banking licence, as the case may be,

then, on and from the relevant day, any such condition shall be deemed to be a condition attached to that banking licence, registration or restricted banking licence, as the case may be, as if, on the relevant day, the Monetary Authority had attached such condition under section 16 to that banking licence, registration or restricted banking licence, as the case may be, and notwithstanding that the term "authorization" is used in section 16(1)(a) and (5), and the provisions of this Ordinance shall apply accordingly.

(6) Where any former registration or former restricted banking licence which is, on and from the relevant day, deemed by virtue of subsection (3) to be registration or a restricted banking licence, as the case may be, was, immediately before the relevant day, suspended under Part VI, then, on and from the relevant day, that registration or restricted banking licence, as the case may be, shall, in the like manner, be deemed to be suspended under that Part for the period concerned of such suspension left to serve immediately before the relevant day as if, on the relevant day and for that period, the Monetary Authority had under that Part suspended that registration or restricted banking licence, as the case may be, and notwithstanding that the term "authorization" is used in that Part, and the provisions of this Ordinance shall apply accordingly.

(7) Where-

> *(a)* immediately before the relevant day, there was in existence an application under Part VII for the transfer of any former banking licence, former registration or former restricted banking licence from an authorized institution to another person in relation to which the designated authority within the meaning of that Part had not granted or refused such transfer; and

> *(b)* on and from the relevant day, that former banking licence, former registration or former restricted banking licence is deemed by virtue of subsection (3) to be a banking licence, registration or restricted banking licence, as the case may be,

then, on and from the relevant day, that application shall be deemed to be an application under Part VII to the Monetary Authority for such transfer, and notwithstanding that the term "authorization" is used in Part VII, and the provisions of this Ordinance shall apply accordingly.

(8) Where-

> *(a)* an act, matter or thing has been done or deemed to be done under Part X as in force at any time before the relevant day by the Monetary Authority, the Financial Secretary or the Governor in Council to or in relation to an authorized institution; and

> *(b)* on and from the relevant day, the former banking licence, former registration or former restricted banking licence held by that institution is deemed by virtue of subsection (3) to be a

banking licence, registration or restricted banking licence, as the case may be,

then, on and from the relevant day, to the extent that but for the enactment of the relevant Ordinance that act, matter or thing would on or after the relevant day have had any force or effect or been in operation, that act, matter or thing shall, in the like manner, and subject to such modifications as may be necessary, be deemed to have been done under Part X by the Monetary Authority, the Financial Secretary or the Governor in Council, as the case may be, to or in relation to the bank, deposit-taking company or restricted licence bank, as the case may be, which holds that banking licence, registration or restricted banking licence, as the case may be, as if, on the relevant day, that act, matter or thing were, to that extent, done under Part X by the Monetary Authority, the Financial Secretary or the Governor in Council, as the case may be, to or in relation to that bank, deposit-taking company or restricted licence bank, as the case may be, and the provisions of this Ordinance shall apply accordingly.

(9) To the extent that any of the other provisions of this Part have any force or effect or are in operation on or after the relevant day, they shall be read, and have such force or effect or operation, as the case may be, subject to such modifications as are necessary to take into account the provisions of this section.

FIRST SCHEDULE

[ss. 2(1), 12(3), 14(1) & 135(1)]

Specified Period And Specified Sums

1. 3 months.

2. The sum for the purposes of section 14(1)(a) is $100,000 or an equivalent amount in any other currency.

3. Sum for the purposes of section 14(1)(b) is $500,000 or an equivalent

amount in any other currency.

SECOND SCHEDULE

[ss. 19, 23, 26, 27, 45, 48, 51, 109, 135(2) & 144]

Fees

$

1.	Banking licence fee (section 19(1))	474,340
1A.	Renewal of banking licence fee (section 19(2))	474,340
2.	Registration fee (section 19(1))	113,020
3.	Renewal of registration fee (section 19(2))	113,020
4.	Restricted banking licence fee (section 19(1))	384,270
5.	Renewal of restricted banking licence fee (section 19(2))	384,270
6.	Inspection fee (section 20(5))	10
7.	Fee for a copy or extract, per page (section 20(5))	5
8.	Fee for the establishment of a local branch of a bank, other than a restricted licence bank (section 45(1))	22,400
9.	Annual fee for maintaining a local branch of a bank, other than a restricted licence bank (section 45(1) and (2))	22,400
10.	Fee for the establishment of a local branch of a restricted licence bank or deposit-taking company (section 45(1))	19,110
11.	Annual fee for maintaining a local branch of a restricted licence bank or deposit-taking company (section 45(1) and (2))	19,110
12.	Fee for the establishment of a local representative office (section 48(1))	22,400
13.	Annual fee for maintaining a local representative office (section 48(1), (2) and (3))	22,400

14. Fee for the establishment of an overseas branch of a bank, other than a restricted licence bank (section 51(1)) 44,800

15. Annual fee for maintaining an overseas branch of a bank, other than a restricted licence bank (section 51(1) and (2)) 44,800

16. Fee for the establishment of an overseas branch of a restricted licence bank or deposit-taking company (section 51(1)) 38,400

17. Annual fee for maintaining an overseas branch of a restricted licence bank or deposit-taking company (section 51 (1) and (2)) 38,400

18. Fee for the establishment of an overseas representative office of a bank, other than a restricted licence bank (section 51(1)) 11,200

19. Annual fee for maintaining an overseas representative office of a bank, other than a restricted licence bank (section 51(1) and (2))11,200

20. Fee for the establishment of an overseas representative office of a restricted licence bank or deposit-taking company (section 51(1)) 19,110

21. Annual fee for maintaining an overseas representative office of a restricted licence bank or deposit-taking company (section 51(1) and (2)) 19,110

THIRD SCHEDULE

[ss. 98 & 135(3)]

Capital Adequacy Ratio

1. In this Schedule-

"bank" means-

(a) any authorized institution (other than any authorized institution the authorization of which is for the time being suspended under section 24 or 25 of this Ordinance); and

(b) any bank incorporated outside Hong Kong which is not an authorized institution, except such a bank-

(i) which, in the opinion of the Monetary Authority, is not adequately supervised by the relevant banking supervisory authority; or

(ii) the licence or other authorization of which to carry on banking business is for the time being suspended;

"book value" in relation to any thing means its current book value after deducting the amount of any specific provision made in the books against a reduction in its value;

"capital base" means the capital base of an authorized institution determined in accordance with paragraph 3;

"Claims on or claims guaranteed by, authorized institutions in Hong Kong" do not include any claim on or guarantee by an authorized institution the authorization of which is for the time being suspended under this Ordinance;

"Core Capital" means the sum, calculated in Hong Kong dollars, of the book values of the capital items listed in paragraph 3(a) to (f);

"debt securities" means securities other than shares or stocks;

"external sovereign debt" means cross-border debt contracted by, or guaranteed by, a central government including any cross-border debt contracted by, or guaranteed by, commercial or other non-central government entities where there are factors indicative of a general inability

for such entities to comply with their debt terms due to the unavailability of foreign currency, central government restrictions or regulations, or any other factor indicative of severe transfer risk problems;

"gold bullion held on an allocated basis" means gold bullion held by a person other than the authorized institution, to the order of the authorized institution, and which is separately ascertainable;

"guarantee" includes indemnity;

"multilateral development bank" means the International Bank for Reconstruction and Development, the Inter-American Development Bank, the Asian Development Bank, the African Development Bank, the European Investment Bank, the Nordic Investment Bank, the Caribbean Development Bank, the European Bank for Reconstruction and Development or the

International Finance Corporation;

"public sector entity in Hong Kong" means the Mass Transit Railway Corporation, the Kowloon-Canton Railway Corporation, the Hong Kong Housing Authority and any body specified by the Monetary Authority in a notice published in the Gazette;

"public sector entity of any other Tier 1 country" means an entity which is regarded as a public sector entity by a recognized banking supervisory authority in the place in which it is incorporated;

"residential mortgage" means a mortgage under which-

   (a)   the borrower is an individual person;

   (b)   the principal sum does not exceed 90% of the purchase price or the market value of the property, whichever amount is the lower;

   (c)   the debt is secured by a first legal charge on the property;

   (d)   the property secured by the charge is used as the borrower's residence or as a residence by a tenant of the borrower;

"risk weighted exposure" means the risk weighted exposure of an authorized institution determined in accordance with paragraph 4;

"Supplementary Capital" means the sum, calculated in Hong Kong dollars, of the book values of the capital items listed in paragraph 3(g) to (o) calculated in accordance with that paragraph;

"Tier 1 country" means a country which is a member of the Organization for Economic Co-operation and Development or a country which has concluded a special lending arrangement with the International Monetary Fundassociated with the Fund's General Arrangements to Borrow, and also includes Hong Kong but excludes any country which has rescheduled its external sovereign debt, whether to central government or non-central government creditors, within the previous 5 years;

"Tier 2 country" means any country which is not a Tier 1 country;

"valid bilateral netting agreement" means a bilateral netting agreement in respect of which the following conditions are satisfied-

   (a)   the bilateral netting agreement is in writing;

   (b)   the bilateral netting agreement creates a single legal obligation for all individual contracts covered by the agreement, and provides, in effect, that the authorized institution would have a

single claim or obligation either to receive or pay only the net amount of the sum of the positive and negative mark-to-market values of the individual contracts covered by the agreement in the event that a counterparty to the agreement, or a counterparty to whom the agreement has been validly assigned, fails to comply with any obligation under that agreement due to default, insolvency, bankruptcy, or similar circumstance;

(c)   the authorized institution has been given legal advice to the effect that in the event of a challenge in a court of law, including a challenge resulting from default, insolvency, bankruptcy, or similar circumstance, the relevant court or administrative authority would find the authorized institution's exposure to be the net amount under-

   (i)   the law of Hong Kong or, in the case of a subsidiary of the authorized institution which is incorporated outside Hong Kong and which is included in the calculation of the capital adequacy ratio of the institution on a consolidated basis, the law of the jurisdiction in which the subsidiary is incorporated;

   (ii)   the law of the jurisdiction in which the counterparty is incorporated or the equivalent location in the case of non-corporate entities, and if a branch of the counterparty is involved, then also under the law of the jurisdiction in which the branch is located;

   (iii)   the law that governs the individual contracts covered by the bilateral netting agreement; and

   (iv)   the law that governs the bilateral netting agreement;

(d)   the authorized institution establishes and maintains procedures to monitor developments in any law relevant to the bilateral netting agreement and to ensure that the bilateral netting agreement continues to satisfy the conditions applicable to this definition;

(e)   the authorized institution manages the transactions covered by the bilateral netting agreement on a net basis;

(f)   the authorized institution maintains in its files documentation adequate to support the netting of the contracts covered by the bilateral netting agreement; and

(g)   the bilateral netting agreement is not subject to a provision that permits the non-defaulting counterparty to make only limited payment, or no payment at all, to the defaulter or the estate of the defaulter, regardless of whether or not the defaulter is a net creditor under the agreement.

2.   The capital adequacy ratio of an authorized institution shall be calculated as the ratio, expressed as a percentage, of its capital base, determined in accordance with paragraph 3, to its risk weighted exposure determined in accordance with paragraph 4.

3.   The capital base of an authorized institution shall be determined by taking the sum, calculated in Hong Kong dollars, of the book values (except in relation to subparagraph (i), where the difference between the market value and the book value is to be taken) of-

Category I - Core Capital

(a)   its paid-up ordinary share capital;

(b)   its paid-up, irredeemable, non-cumulative preference shares, that is to say, shares that are irredeemable or that may be redeemed only with the prior consent of the Monetary Authority;

(c)   its share premium account;

(d)   its reserves other than those referred to in subparagraphs (e), (g), (h) and (i);

(e)   its profit and loss account including its current year's profit or loss;

(f)   where the Monetary Authority requires under section 79A (1) a provision of Part XV to apply to the authorized institution on a consolidated basis, or requires under section 98(2) the capital adequacy ratio of the authorized institution to be calculated on a consolidated basis, minority interests arising on such consolidation in the equity of its subsidiaries:

Provided that the amount to be included as Core Capital shall be determined by deducting therefrom the book value calculated in Hong Kong dollars of the goodwill of the institution; Category II-Supplementary Capital

(g)   its inner reserves;

(h)   its reserves on revaluation of its real property, but not exceeding 70% of any surplus on revaluation;

(i)   its latent reserves (i.e. the difference between the market value and the book value) determined upon revaluation, of long-term holding of equity securities listed on the Unified Exchange or on any exchange referred to in the Schedule to the *Securities (Specification of Approved Assets, Liquid Assets and Ranking Liabilities) Notice 1990 (Cap. 333 sub. leg.):

Provided that-

(i)   the amount of any increase in value to be included shall be limited to 45% of such increase;

(ii)   the amount of any diminution in value is deducted;

(j)   its general provisions against doubtful debts but not including any provisions against specified or identified losses and against the diminution in the value of particular assets:

Provided that the amount included under this subparagraph may not exceed 1.25% of the figure derived by the calculation specified in subparagraph (a) of paragraph 4 carried out in relation to the authorized institution;

(k)   its perpetual subordinated debt where the Monetary Authority is satisfied that under the terms of the debt instrument the following conditions are met-

(i)   the claims of the lender against the authorized institution are fully subordinated to those of all unsubordinated creditors;

(ii)   the debt is not secured against any assets of the authorized institution;

(iii)   the money advanced to the authorized institution is permanently available to it;

(iv)   the debt is not repayable without the prior consent of the Monetary Authority;

(v)   the money advanced to the authorized institution is available to meet losses without the institution being obliged to cease trading;

(vi)   the authorized institution is entitled to defer the payment of interest where its profitability will not support such payment;

(l)   its paid-up irredeemable cumulative preference shares, that is to say, shares that are irredeemable or that may be redeemed only with the prior consent of the Monetary Authority;

(m)   its term subordinated debt, where the Monetary Authority is satisfied that under the terms of the debt instrument the following conditions are met-

(i)   the claims of the lender against the authorized institution are fully subordinated to those of all unsubordinated creditors;

(ii)   the debt is not secured against any assets of the authorized institution;

(iii)   the debt has a minimum initial period to maturity of more than 5 years (and notwithstanding that that period may be reduced with the prior consent of the Monetary Authority);

(iv)   where the debt is repaid prior to maturity, the debt is not repayable without the prior consent of the Monetary Authority:

Provided that-

(A)   amounts included under this subparagraph shall be discounted by 20% each year during the 4 years immediately preceding maturity; and

(B)   the total amount included under this subparagraph and subparagraph (n) shall not exceed in total, 50% of the total of the Core Capital;

(n)   its paid-up term preference shares, where the Monetary Authority is satisfied that the shares have been issued and remain subject to the following conditions-

(i)   the shares have a minimum initial period to maturity of more than 5 years;

(ii)   the shares are not redeemable without the prior consent of the Monetary Authority:

Provided that-

(A)   amounts included under this subparagraph shall be discounted by 20% of the original amount each year during the 4 years immediately preceding maturity; and

(B)   the total amount included under this subparagraph and subparagraph (m) shall not exceed in total, 50% of the total of the Core Capital; and

(o)   where the Monetary Authority requires under section 79A(1) a provision of Part XV to apply to the authorized institution on a consolidated basis, or requires under section 98(2) the capital adequacy ratio of the authorized institution to be calculated on a consolidated basis, any minority interests arising on such consolidation in the paid-up irredeemable cumulative preference shares and paid-up term preference shares of its subsidiaries:

Provided that the amount to be included as Supplementary Capital shall not exceed the total of the amount determined as Core Capital,

and by deducting therefrom the sum calculated in Hong Kong dollars of the book value of-

(A)   its shareholding in any company which is a subsidiary or holding company of the authorized institution, other than-

(i)   any shareholding that falls to be deducted under subparagraph (B), (C) or (D); and

(ii)   where the Monetary Authority requires under section 79A(1) a provision of Part XV to apply to the authorized institution on a consolidated basis, or requires under section 98(2) the capital adequacy ratio of the authorized institution to be calculated on a consolidated basis, its shareholding in any subsidiary the subject of such consolidation;

(B)   its loans to, shares and debentures issued by, and its guarantees

of the liabilities of, connected companies of the authorized institution (other than shares that fall to be deducted under subparagraph (D)), where in the opinion of the Monetary Authority the institution has made the loans, is holding the shares or debentures or, as the case may be, has given the guarantees, other than in the ordinary course of business; and for the purposes of this subparagraph "shares" and "debentures" mean shares and debentures within the meaning of section 2(1) of the Companies Ordinance (Cap.32), and a company shall be treated as a connected company of the institution if it is a subsidiary or the holding company of the institution, or is otherwise of a description falling within section 64(1)(b), (c), (d) or (e);

(C)   its shareholding in any company in which the authorized institution is entitled to exercise, or control the exercise of, more than 20% of the voting power at general meetings of the company; and

(D)   its holding of shares, stocks or debt securities issued by any bank unless the Monetary Authority is satisfied that the holding is not the subject of an arrangement in which 2 or more persons agree to hold each other's capital or is not otherwise a strategic investment.

4.   The risk weighted exposure of an authorized institution shall be that figure derived by-

    (a)   adding together all the products achieved by-

        (i)   taking the book value, calculated in Hong Kong dollars, of each of the items referred to in Table A in relation to the authorized institution; and, in relation to each item multiplying that value by the risk weight specified in Table A in relation to that item; and

        (ii)   multiplying the credit equivalent amount of each of the items referred to in Table B by the appropriate risk weight specified in Table A as if the items to which they relate were on-balance sheet (Table A) items provided that in relation to items 12 and 13 referred to in Table B, the risk weight shall not exceed 50%. The credit equivalent amount may be obtained-

            (A)   in relation to items 12 and 13 referred to in Table B where the current exposure method of valuation is used, by adding-

(I) the current exposure, which, in the case of exchange rate and interest rate contracts not covered by a valid bilateral netting agreement is the sum of the positive mark-to-market values, calculated in Hong Kong dollars, of the contracts; and in the case of exchange rate and interest rate contracts covered by a valid bilateral netting agreement is the net amount, if positive, of the sum of the positive and negative mark-to-market values, calculated in Hong Kong dollars, of each contract covered by the agreement; and

(II) the potential future credit exposure of exchange rate contracts and interest rate contracts derived by multiplying the principal amount of each contract by the credit conversion factor specified in items 12(b) and 13(h) of Table B;

(B) in any case apart from those mentioned in sub-sub-subparagraph (A), including in relation to

items 12 and 13 referred to in Table B where the original exposure method of valuation is used, by taking the principal amount, calculated in Hong Kong dollars, of each of the items referred to in Table B in relation to the authorized institution and multiplying the principal amount by the credit conversion factor specified in Table B in relation to that item; and

(b) subtracting from the sum calculated under subparagraph (a) the value of general provisions not included in the capital base of the authorized institution.

TABLE A - ON-BALANCE SHEET ITEMS

Category I - Cash items

Item	Nature of item	Risk weight
1.	Notes and coins.	0%
2.	Hong Kong Government certificates of indebtedness.	0%
3.	Gold bullion in the possession of an authorized institution or held on an allocated basis, to the extent backed by gold liabilities.	0%
4.	Gold held which is not backed by gold liabilities.	100%
5.	Claims to the extent that they are collateralized by cash deposits held by the authorized institution.	0%
6.	Cash items in the course of collection.	20%
6A.	Amounts due from the sale of securities, where the authorized institution has executed the transaction on behalf of a customer or for its own account, up to and including the fifth working day after the due settlement date in respect of the transaction.	0%
6B.	Amounts due from the purchase of securities, where the authorized institution has executed the transaction on behalf of a customer, up to and including the fifth working day after the due settlement date in respect of the transaction.	0%

Category II - Claims on central governments and central banks

Item	Nature of item	Risk weight
7.	Loans to, or loans to the extent that they are guaranteed by, the Exchange Fund.	0%
8.	Loans to, or loans to the extent that they are guaranteed by, the central government or the central bank of any Tier 1 country.	0%

9.   Holdings of fixed interest securities with a residual maturity of under 1 year or floating rate securities of any maturity issued by or guaranteed by the central government or by the central bank of a Tier 1 country, or by the Exchange Fund, or claims to the extent that they are collateralized by such securities.   10%

10.   Holdings of fixed interest securities with a residual maturity of 1 year and over issued by or guaranteed by the central government or by the central bank of a Tier 1 country, or by the Exchange Fund, or claims to the extent that they are collateralized by such securities.   20%

11.   Loans denominated in the currency of a Tier 2 country and funded in that currency, to, or to the extent that they are guaranteed by, the central government or the central bank of that country.   0%

12.   Holdings of fixed interest securities with a residual maturity of under 1 year or floating rate securities of any maturity issued by or guaranteed by the central government or by the central bank of a Tier 2 country, where denominated and funded in the currency of that country.   10%

13.   Holdings of fixed interest securities with a residual maturity of 1 year and over issued by or guaranteed by the central government or by the central bank of a Tier 2 country, where denominated and funded in the currency of that country.   20%

14.   Other claims on the central government or on the central bank of a Tier 2 country.   100%

Category III - Claims on Public Sector Entities

Item	Nature of item	Risk weight
15.	Claims on or to the extent that they are guaranteed by, public sector entities in Hong Kong.	20%
16.	Claims on or to the extent that they are guaranteed by, public sector entities of any other Tier 1 country.	20%
17.	Claims on public sector entities of a Tier 2 country.	100%

Category IV- Claims on banks

Item	Nature of item	Risk weight
18.	Claims on or to the extent that they are guaranteed by, authorized institutions or banks incorporated in Tier 1 countries.	20%
19.	Claims on or to the extent that they are guaranteed or collateralized by securities issued by, a multilateral development bank.	20%
20.	Claims on or to the extent that they are guaranteed by, any bank other than a bank referred to in item 18 or 19, with a residual maturity of under 1 year.	20%
21.	Claims on or to the extent that they are guaranteed by, any bank other than a bank referred to in item 18 or 19, with a residual maturity of 1 year or more.	100%

Category V- Residential Mortgages

Item	Nature of item	Risk weight
22.	Loans fully secured by a residential mortgage.	50%
23.	Securities backed by residential mortgages and participations in residential mortgages.	50%

Category VI - Other assets

Item	Nature of item	Risk weight
24.	Claims on non-bank private sector persons.	100%
25.	Investments in the equity or other capital instruments of other banks, other than where deducted from the capital base.	100%
26.	Premises, plant and equipment and other fixed assets for the authorized institution's own use.	100%
27.	Other interests in real property.	100%
28.	All assets not elsewhere specified.	100%

TABLE B - OFF-BALANCE SHEET ITEMS

Item	Nature of item	Credit conversion factor
1.	**Direct credit substitutes**	
	Irrevocable off-balance sheet obligations which carry the same credit risk as a direct extension of credit. This includes guarantees, the confirming of letters of credit, standby letters of credit serving as financial guarantees for loans, securities and acceptances (including endorsements with the character of acceptances) other than acceptances included in item 3.	100%
2.	**Transaction-related contingencies** Contingent liabilities which involve an irrevocable obligation of the authorized institution to pay a beneficiary when a customer fails to perform some contractual, non-financial obligation. This includes performance bonds, bid bonds, warranties and standby letters of credit related to a particular transaction.	50%
3.	**Trade-related contingencies** Contingent liabilities which relate to trade related obligations. This includes letters of credit, acceptances on trade bills, shipping guarantees and any other trade related contingencies.	20%
4.	**Sale and repurchase agreements (see Note 1)** Arrangements whereby the authorized institution sells a loan, security or other asset to another person with a commitment to repurchase the asset at an agreed price on an agreed future date.	100%
5.	**Assets sales or other transactions with recourse (see Note 1)** Assets sales where the holder of the asset is entitled to put the asset back to the authorized institution within an agreed period or should the value or credit quality of the asset deteriorate.	100%
6.	**Forward asset purchases (see Note 1)** Commitment to purchase a loan, security or other asset, including under a put option granted by the authorized institution to another party, at specified future date on pre-arranged terms.	100%
7.	**Partly paid-up shares and securities (held by the authorized institution)** The unpaid portion of shares or securities which the issuer of such shares or securities may call for at a future date.	100%
8.	**Forward forward deposits placed**	

Any agreement between the authorized institution and another party whereby the institution will place a deposit at an agreed rate of interest with that party at some predetermined future date. 100%

9. Note issuance and revolving underwriting facilities
Arrangements whereby a borrower may draw down funds up to a prescribed limit over a predefined period by making repeated note issues to the market, and where, should the issue prove unable to be placed in the market, the unplaced amount is to be taken up or funds made available by the underwriter of the facility. 50%

10. Other commitments with an original maturity of under 1 year or which may be cancelled at any time unconditionally by the authorized institution. 0%

11. Other commitments with an original maturity of 1 year or over. 50%

12. Exchange rate contracts (see Note 2) (Calculated in accordance with either the original exposure method or the current exposure method)

(a) credit conversion factors to be used in calculating in accordance with original exposure method (see Note 3)- contracts with an original maturity of-

(i) under 1 year; 2%

(ii) 1 year and less than 2 years; 5%

(iii) 2 years or more, the factor for 1 year and less than 2 years plus for each additional year; 3%

(b) credit conversion factors to be used to determine the potential future credit exposure in accordance with the current exposure method- contracts with a residual maturity of-

(i) under 1 year; 1%

(ii) 1 year and over. 5%

13. Interest rate contracts (see Note 2) (Calculated in accordance with either the original exposure method or the current exposure method) *(a)* credit conversion factors to be used in calculating in accordance with the original exposure method (see Note 3) -

contracts with an original maturity of-

(i) under 1 year; 0.5%

(ii) 1 year and under 2 years; 1%

(iii) 2 years or more, the factor for 1 year and under 2 years plus for each additional year; 1%

(b) credit conversion factors to be used to determine the potential future credit exposure in accordance with the current exposure method-
contracts with a residual maturity of-

(i) under 1 year; 0%

(ii) 1 year and over. 0.5%

Note

1. The appropriate risk weight to be used in relation to transactions to which items 4, 5 and 6 apply, shall be determined on the basis of the nature of the asset and not the nature of the counterparty with whom the transaction has been entered into.

Reverse repos (i.e. purchase and resale agreements where the authorized institution is the recipient of the asset) are to be regarded as collateralized loans.

2. In relation to exchange rate contracts and interest rate contracts an authorized institution shall, in determining the credit equivalent amount use either the current exposure method of valuation or, with the agreement of the Monetary Authority, the original exposure method of valuation.

3. If an authorized institution nets its obligation with a counterparty under a valid bilateral netting agreement, it may use the following credit conversion factor-

Banking Ordinance

	Nature of item	Credit conversion factor

1. Exchange rate contracts

Credit conversion factors to be used in calculating
contracts with an original maturity of-

(a)	under 1 year	1.5%
(b)	1 year and under 2 years	3.75%
(c)	2 years of more, the factor for 1 year and under 2 years plus for each additional year	2.25%

2. Interest rate contracts

Credit conversion factors to be used in calculating contracts with an original maturity of -

(a)	under 1 year	0.35%
(b)	1 year and under 2 years	0.75%
(c)	2 years of more, the factor for 1 year and under 2 years plus for each additional year	0.75%

FOURTH SCHEDULE

[ss. 102 & 135(3)]

Liquidity Ratio

1.　　In this Schedule-

"debt securities" means any securities other than shares, stocks, import or export trade bills;

"eligible loan repayment" means a repayment to an authorized institution by a customer other than a relevant bank in respect of a loan-

　　　(a)　　which the authorized institution is not committed to continue, by renewal or otherwise; and

　　　(b)　　which is fully performing,

being a repayment-

　　　(i)　　the date of which is fixed;

　　　(ii)　　which will fall due within 1 month; and

　　　(iii)　　in respect of which the authorized institution has no reason to expect a default,

and where the loan is secured by a deposit referred to in paragraph 7-

　　　(A)　　in the case where the loan will be fully repaid after receiving the repayment, only that part of the repayment that exceeds the aggregate of the deposit and interest payable on the deposit shall be taken to be eligible loan repayment;

　　　(B)　　in the case where the loan will not be so fully repaid, the repayment so far as it is not made by a corresponding reduction of the amount of the deposit or interest payable on the deposit or both shall be taken to be eligible loan repayment;

"marketable debt securities" means debt securities which have an established secondary market in Hong Kong or elsewhere in which they can be sold readily;

"multilateral development bank" has the meaning assigned to it in the

Third Schedule;

"one-month liability", in relation to any authorized institution or relevant bank, means-

    (a)   any liability, other than a contingent liability, the effect of which will or could be to reduce within 1 month the liquefiable assets of that authorized institution or relevant bank; and

    (b)   any contingent liability that in the opinion of the Monetary Authority may result in a reduction within 1 month of the liquefiable assets of that authorized institution or relevant bank;

"principal amount"-

    (a)   in relation to gold or a marketable debt security or prescribed instrument, means the lower of the market value and the book value of the asset;

    (b)   in relation to any other liquefiable asset set out in Table A or a liability set out in Table B, means the book value of the asset or liability, and for this purpose, book value shall include interest receivable or payable by an authorized institution on the asset or liability, where applicable,

at the close of business on a working day;

"public sector entity in Hong Kong" has the meaning assigned to it in the Third Schedule;

"qualifying credit rating" means either-

    (a)   a credit rating appraised by a credit rating agency set out in column 1 of the following Table and which is not lower than-

        (i)   in the case of long-term rating, the rating specified in column 2 in relation to that credit rating agency; and

        (ii)   in the case of short-term rating, the rating specified in column 3 in relation to that credit rating agency:

TABLE

Column 1	Column 2	Column 3
Credit rating agency	Long-term rating	Short-term rating
Moody's Investors Service, Inc.	A3	Prime-1
Standard and Poor's Corporation	A-	A- 1;

or

(b)   a rating appraised by a credit rating agency approved by the Monetary Authority and considered by him as a rating equivalent to a rating in that Table;

"relevant bank" means-

(a)   any authorized institution other than an institution the authorization of which is for the time being suspended under section 24 or 25 of this Ordinance; or

(b)   any bank incorporated outside Hong Kong which is not an authorized institution, except such a bank-

     (i)   which, in the opinion of the Monetary Authority, is not adequately supervised by the relevant banking supervisory authority; or

     (ii)   the licence or other authorization of which to carry on banking business is for the time being suspended,

and includes the Exchange Fund established by the Exchange Fund Ordinance (Cap. 66).

2.   The liquidity ratio of an authorized institution shall be calculated-

(a)   as the ratio, expressed as a percentage, of the net weighted amount of its liquefiable assets determined in accordance with

paragraph 4, to its qualifying liabilities, as determined in accordance with paragraph 6; and

(b)   for each calendar month, on the basis of the sum of the net weighted amount of the liquefiable assets and the sum of the qualifying liabilities for each working day of that month.

3. Notwithstanding paragraph 2(b), the Monetary Authority may, as he thinks fit, by notice in writing served on an authorized institution, permit the authorized institution to calculate its liquidity ratio by reference to such days during the month as the Monetary Authority may specify in the notice (and, if any such specified day is a public holiday, the immediately preceding working day shall be taken for the purpose of such calculation).

4. Subject to paragraph 9, the net weighted amount of the liquefiable assets of an authorized institution shall be the difference between the total of the weighted amounts calculated in accordance with paragraph 5 of each item specified in Table A held by the authorized institution that meets the requirements of paragraph 8 and the weighted amount calculated in accordance with paragraph 5 of the item specified in Table B.

5. The weighted amount of an item in Table A or B shall be calculated, in Hong Kong dollars, by multiplying the principal amount of that item by the liquidity conversion factor specified in column 3 in Table A or B in relation to that item.

6. The qualifying liabilities of an authorized institution shall be the sum, calculated in Hong Kong dollars and at book value, of-

(a)   the amount, if any, by which the total one-month liabilities of relevant banks to the authorized institution are exceeded by its total one-month liabilities to relevant banks; and

(b)   the total of its other one-month liabilities,

at the close of business on a working day and for this purpose, interest payable by the authorized institution and the relevant banks shall be included in the calculation of the liabilities.

7. A deposit which has been pledged with an authorized institution for securing a loan granted to a customer other than a relevant bank and the deposit would otherwise be included in the calculation of qualifying liabilities under paragraph 6 shall be excluded in the calculation to the extent of the outstanding balance of the loan.

8. The requirements for a liquefiable asset referred to in paragraph 4 are-

(a)   except in the case described in paragraph 11(a), it must not be overdue;

201

(b)   it must be free from encumbrances;

(c)   it must be freely remittable and payable to the authorized institution concerned;

(d)   it must be denominated in Hong Kong dollars or in a currency freely convertible into Hong Kong dollars.

9. The Monetary Authority may, for the purpose of calculating the liquidity ratio of an authorized institution, exclude-

(a)   as a liquefiable asset, any asset or class of assets which is, in his opinion, not capable of generating cash or cash equivalent within 1 month; and

(b)   from Table B, any debt security or prescribed instrument, subject to the Monetary Authority being satisfied with the treatment of the security or instrument for the purpose of the calculation of qualifying liabilities.

10. For the purpose of the definition of "eligible loan repayment", a loan shall be regarded as fully performing if-

(a)   there are no arrears of principal or interest payment in respect of the loan; and

(b)   the loan is not a loan-

      (i)   that has been raised to repay another loan granted to the same customer by the authorized institution; or

      (ii)   the repayment date or dates of which have been postponed.

11. Notwithstanding paragraph 10-

(a)   the requirement of paragraph 10(a) may be regarded as met in the case where the loan is repayable by periodic instalments at intervals of not more than 1 month and there is no instalment which is in arrears for more than 1 month on the working day concerned; and

(b)   a loan of the type described in paragraph 10(b)(i) or (ii) may be regarded as fully performing if-

(i)   the raising of the loan or the postponement of the repayment date or dates was not caused by a deterioration in the financial position of the customer or by his inability to repay on the original repayment date or dates;

(ii)   the new or revised repayment terms are not unfavourable to the authorized institution as compared to the terms of other loans of similar nature granted by the authorized institution to other customers and negotiated at arm's length, and

(iii)   the loan meets the requirement of paragraph 10(a).

TABLE A

Item	Liquefiable assets	Liquidity conversion factor
1. Currency notes and coins		100%
2. Gold		100%
3. The amount, if any, by which the total one-month liabilities of the authorized institution to relevant banks are exceeded by the total one-month liabilities of relevant banks to it		100%
4. Export bills-		
	(a) payable within 1 month and which are either drawn under letters of credit issued by relevant banks or accepted and payable by relevant banks; or	100%
	(b) covered by irrevocable re-discounting facilities approved by the Monetary Authority	100%
5. Marketable debt securities or prescribed instruments-		
	(a) issued or guaranteed by-	
	(i) the Hong Kong Government,	

the Exchange Fund, a public sector
entity in Hong Kong or multilateral
development bank with a remaining
term to maturity of-

(A)	not more than 1 year	100%
(B)	more than 1 year	95%

    (ii)   an authorized institution incorporated
in Hong Kong or the Hong Kong branch
of an authorized institution incorporated
overseas with a remaining term to maturity of-

(A)	not more than 1 month	100%
(B)	more than 1 month but not more than 1 year	95%
C)	more than 1 year	90%

    (b)   with a qualifying credit rating, issued or
guaranteed by-

    (i)   the central bank or central government
of any country with a remaining term to
maturity of-

(A)	not more than 1 year	100%
(B)	more than 1 year	95%

(See Note 1)

    (ii)   a relevant bank, other than one referred
to in paragraph (a)(ii), with a remaining
term to maturity of-

(A)	not more than 1 month	100%
(B)	more than 1 month but not more than 1 year	95%
(C)	more than 1 year	90%

(iii) a regional government of any country or other institution with a remaining term to maturity of-

    (A) not more than 1 year   90%

    (B) more than 1 year but not more than 5 years   85%

    (C) more than 5 years   80%

(c) without a qualifying credit rating, issued or guaranteed by a relevant bank, other than one referred to in paragraph (a)(ii), with a remaining term to maturity of not more than 1 month   100%

(d) approved for inclusion by the Monetary Authority   80%

(e) not included elsewhere in this item with a remaining term to maturity of not more than 1 month   80%

6. Eligible loan repayments   80%

Note 1

Item 5(b)(i) includes a marketable debt security or prescribed instrument which does not have a credit rating but which is issued or guaranteed by the central bank or central government of a country that has a qualifying credit rating.

TABLE B

Item	Liquefiable assets	Liquidity conversion factor
1.	Debt securities or prescribed instruments with a remaining term to maturity of not more than 1 month issued by the authorized institution	100%

FIFTH SCHEDULE

[ss. 92(5)(c) &(7) & 135(3)]

REQUIREMENTS APPLICABLE TO PRESCRIBED

ADVERTISEMENTS

Interpretation

1.(1) In this Schedule-

"deposit-taker", in relation to a prescribed advertisement, means the person with whom the deposits which are invited by the advertisement are to be

made;

"full name", in relation to a person, means the name under which that person carries on business and, if different and if that person is a body corporate, its corporate name;

"liabilities" includes provisions where such provisions have not been deducted from the value of assets.

(2) A reference in this Schedule to the payment of interest in respect of a deposit includes a reference to the payment of any premium in respect of the deposit, and to the crediting of interest to the deposit so as to constitute an accretion to the principal.

(3) For the purposes of this Schedule, a prescribed advertisement which contains information which is intended or might reasonably be presumed to be intended to lead directly or indirectly to the making of a deposit shall be treated as if it contained an invitation to make a deposit, and references to an invitation to make a deposit shall be construed accordingly.

Warning

2. Every prescribed advertisement shall contain a prominent warning to the effect that the deposit-taker is not an authorized institution within the meaning of this Ordinance and is therefore not subject to the supervision of the Monetary
Authority.

General requirements for prescribed advertisements

3.   Every prescribed advertisement shall state-

   (a)   the full name of the deposit-taker;

   (b)   the country or territory in which the deposit-taker's principal place of business is situated, described as such; and

   (c)   if the deposit-taker is a body corporate, the country or territory in which it is incorporated, described as such, unless this is the same as the country or territory referred to in subparagraph (b).

Assets and liabilities

4.(1)   Every prescribed advertisement shall state the amount of the paid-up capital and reserves, described as such, of the deposit-taker (if a body corporate) or the amount of the total assets less liabilities, described as such, of the deposit-taker (if a person other than a body corporate).

(2) Where a prescribed advertisement contains any reference to the amount of the assets of the deposit-taker, it shall state the total amount of the deposit-taker's liabilities, described as such, which statement shall be not less prominent than such reference.

(3) Subparagraphs (1) and (2) shall be treated as complied with if the prescribed advertisement states that the amount of any assets or paid-up capital and reserves required to be stated exceeds an amount specified in the advertisement or that the amount of any liabilities required to be stated does not exceed an amount so specified.

(4) A prescribed advertisement shall not contain any reference to the assets or liabilities of any person other than the deposit-taker.

Deposit protection arrangements

5. A prescribed advertisement shall not state or imply that the deposits which are invited or their repayment, or interest or the payment of interest in respect of them, will be guaranteed, secured, insured , or the subject of any other form of protection, unless it states-

   (a)   the form of the protection;

   (b)   the extent of the protection; and

   (c)   the full name of the person who will be liable to meet any claim

by the depositor by virtue of the arrangements conferring the protection.

Interest

6.(1) This paragraph applies to a prescribed advertisement which specifies the rate at which interest will be payable in respect of the deposits which are invited.

(2) Every prescribed advertisement to which this paragraph applies shall state-

> *(a)* the minimum amount, if any, which must be deposited to earn that rate of interest;

> *(b)* the period of time, if any, during which no interest will be payable;

> *(c)* the minimum period of time, if any, during which a deposit must be retained by the deposit-taker in order to earn that rate of interest;

> *(d)* the minimum period of notice, if any, which must be given before repayment may be required of a deposit earning that rate of interest; and

> *(e)* the intervals at which the interest will be paid.

(3) If the rate of interest which is specified is not an annual rate of simple interest, the prescribed advertisement shall state the basis on which the rate will be calculated.

(4) If the rate of interest which is specified may be varied during the period for which the deposit will be held this shall be stated in the prescribed advertisement.

(5) If interest will or may not he paid in full at the rate which is specified, this shall be stated in the prescribed advertisement, and the advertisement shall state the nature and the amount of or rate of any deductions which will or may be made from the interest before payment.

(6) If the rate of interest which is specified is or may not be the rate at which interest will be payable in respect of the deposits on the date on which the prescribed advertisement is issued, this shall be stated in the advertisement, and the advertisement shall state the date on which interest was payable at the rate which is specified, such date being as close as is reasonably practicable to the date on which the advertisement is issued.

(7) If the prescribed advertisement specifies more than one rate of interest payable in respect of deposits of a particular amount, the advertisement shall contain the information required by any of subparagraphs (2) to (6) in relation to each such rate.

(8) Where different rates of interest apply to deposits of different amounts, the prescribed advertisement shall contain the information required by any of subparagraphs (2) to (6) in relation to each such rate.

Currency

7. Every prescribed advertisement shall state the currency in which the deposits are to be made.

Supplementary provisions

8.(1) Subject to subparagraph (2), the matters required by this Schedule to be included in a prescribed advertisement shall be shown clearly and legibly or, in the case of an advertisement by way of sound broadcasting, spoken clearly.

(2) In the case of a prescribed advertisement by way of television or exhibition or cinematographic film, the matters required by this Schedule to be included shall be shown clearly and legibly or spoken clearly.

SIXTH SCHEDULE

[s. 137B]

SPECIFIED INSTRUMENTS

1. Any certificate of deposit, being a document-

   (a)   relating to money, in any currency, which has been deposited with the issuer or some other person;

   (b)   which recognizes an obligation to pay a stated amount to bearer, with or without interest; and

   (c)   by the delivery of which, with or without endorsement, the right to receive that stated amount, with or without interest, is transferable.

2. Any instrument, other than a bill of exchange within the meaning of section 3 of the Bills of Exchange Ordinance (Cap. 19) or a promissory note within the meaning of section 89 of the Bills of Exchange Ordinance (Cap. 19), being a document evidencing an obligation to pay a stated or determinable amount to bearer or to order, with or without interest, being an instrument by the delivery of which, with or without endorsement, the right to receive that stated or determinable amount, with or without interest, is transferable.

SEVENTH SCHEDULE

[ss. 16(2) & (10), 17, 29(2) & 135(1) & 8th Sch.]

MINIMUM CRITERIA FOR AUTHORIZATION

1. (1) In this Schedule-

"adequate", in relation to systems of control, includes operating effectively;

"controller" includes a minority shareholder controller;

"net debit balance", in relation to a company, means the aggregate of the excess of accumulated losses over accumulated profits disclosed in the profit and loss account, and other reserves separately disclosed in the balance sheet, of the most recent audited accounts of the company;

"systems of control" includes procedures.

(2) For the purposes of the calculation of the paid-up share capital of a company required by this Schedule, there shall be deducted from such share capital any net debit balance.

(3) For the avoidance of doubt, it is hereby declared that where pursuant to the provisions of this Schedule the Monetary Authority holds an opinion, or is satisfied, in relation to any matter, his holding that opinion or being so satisfied, as the case may be, shall not of itself bind the Monetary Authority-

    (a)   to continue to hold that opinion or to be so satisfied, as the case may be, whether before, on or after the authorization, if any, of the company to which the matter directly or indirectly relates (including any case where that company is seeking a different authorization); or

    (b)   to hold any similar opinion or to be similarly satisfied, as the case may be, in respect of any similar matter which directly or indirectly relates to any other company seeking or having the same or a different authorization from that first-mentioned company.

(4) Without prejudice to the generality of subparagraph (3), the Monetary Authority may regard himself as being satisfied in relation to any matter in respect of which he may be satisfied pursuant to the provisions of this Schedule where-

(a)   the matter directly or indirectly relates to a company incorporated outside Hong Kong;

(b)   the relevant banking supervisory authority informs the Monetary Authority that it is satisfied in relation to that matter; and

(c)   the Monetary Authority is satisfied as to the scope and nature of the supervision exercised by that authority.

(5) For the avoidance of doubt, it is hereby declared that subparagraph (4) shall operate before, on and after the authorization, if any, of the company to which any matter referred to in that subparagraph directly or indirectly relates.

(6) For the purposes of paragraph 13(b)(ii)(A)(VI) and (VII), a company is an associated company of any other company where that second-mentioned company

may-

(a)   by means of the holding of shares or the possession of voting power in or in relation to that first-mentioned company or any other body corporate; or

(b)   by virtue of any powers conferred by the memorandum or articles of association or other document regulating that first-mentioned company or any other body corporate,

significantly influence the conduct of the affairs of that first-mentioned company.

2. If the company is incorporated outside Hong Kong, it is a bank-

(a)   as defined in section 46(9); and

(b)   in respect of which the Monetary Authority is satisfied that it is adequately supervised by the relevant banking supervisory authority.

3. The Monetary Authority is satisfied that he knows the identity of each controller of the company.

4. If the company is incorporated in Hong Kong, the Monetary Authority is satisfied that each person who is, or is to be, a director, controller or chief executive of the company is a fit and proper person to hold the particular position which he holds or is to hold.

5. If the company is incorporated outside Hong Kong, the Monetary Authority is satisfied that each person who is, or is to be-

> (a)   a chief executive of the business in Hong Kong of the company;
>
> (b)   a director, controller or chief executive of the business of the company in the place where it is incorporated,

is a fit and proper person to hold the particular position which he holds or is to hold.

6. The Monetary Authority is satisfied that the company presently has, and will if it is authorized continue to have, adequate financial resources (whether actual or contingent) for the nature and scale of its operations and, without prejudice to the generality of the foregoing-

> (a)   in the case of a company incorporated in Hong Kong seeking authorization to carry on banking business in Hong Kong, its paid-up share capital is not less than $150,000,000 or an equivalent amount in any other approved currency;
>
> (b)   in the case of a company seeking authorization to carry on a deposit-taking business as a deposit-taking company, its paid-up share capital is not less than $25,000,000 or an equivalent amount in any other approved currency;
>
> (c)   in the case of a company seeking authorization to carry on a deposit-taking business as a restricted licence bank, its paid-up share capital is not less than $100,000,000 or an equivalent amount in any other approved currency;
>
> (d)   in the case of a company incorporated in Hong Kong, the company, if it is authorized, will on and after authorization have and maintain a capital adequacy ratio which complies with the provisions of Part XVII applicable to it.

7. The Monetary Authority is satisfied that the company-

> (a)   presently maintains, and will if it is authorized continue to maintain, adequate liquidity to meet its obligations as they will or may fall due; and
>
> (b)   without prejudice to the generality of subparagraph (a), if it is authorized, will on and after authorization have and maintain a liquidity ratio which complies with the provisions of Part XVIII applicable to it.

8. The Monetary Authority is satisfied that the company, if it is authorized, will on and after authorization comply with the provisions of Part XV applicable to it.

9. The Monetary Authority is satisfied that the company presently maintains, and will if it is authorized continue to maintain, adequate provision for depreciation or diminution in the value of its assets (including provision for bad and doubtful debts), for liabilities which will or may fall to be discharged by it and for losses which will or may occur.

10. The Monetary Authority is satisfied that the company presently has, and will if it is authorized continue to have, adequate accounting systems and adequate systems of control.

11. If the company is incorporated in Hong Kong, the Monetary Authority is satisfied that it presently discloses, and will if it is authorized continue to disclose, adequate information-

> *(a)*   in relation to the state of its affairs and its profit and loss; and
>
> *(b)*   in-
>
> > **(i)**   its audited annual accounts within the meaning of section 60(11);
> >
> > **(ii)**   any supplementary information to those audited annual accounts;
> >
> > **(iii)**   the report of the directors under section 129D(1) of the Companies Ordinance (Cap. 32); and
> >
> > **(iv)**   the institution's cash flow statement, together with any notes thereon, where the statement does not already form part of those audited annual accounts.

12. The Monetary Authority is satisfied that the business of the company is presently, and will if it is authorized continue to be, carried on-

> *(a)*   with integrity, prudence and the appropriate degree of professional competence; and
>
> *(b)*   in a manner which is not detrimental, or likely to be detrimental, to the interests of depositors or potential depositors.

13. Where the company is seeking authorization to carry on banking business in Hong Kong-

> *(a)*   in the case of a company incorporated outside Hong Kong-
>
> > **(i)**   either-
> >
> > > **(A)**   the total assets (less contra items) of the whole

banking group of which the company is a part are more than US$16,000,000,000 or an equivalent amount in any other approved currency; or

(B) that, in the opinion of the Monetary Authority, authorizing the company to carry on banking business in Hong Kong would help to promote the interests of Hong Kong as an international financial centre; and

(ii) there is, in the opinion of the Monetary Authority, an acceptable degree of reciprocity in respect of banks incorporated in Hong Kong seeking to carry on banking business in the place where that company is incorporated;

(b) in the case of a company incorporated in Hong Kong-

(i) it is, in the opinion of the Monetary Authority, closely associated and identified with Hong Kong;

(ii) it has-

(A) total deposits from the public of not less than $3,000,000,000, or an equivalent amount in any other approved currency, excluding any deposits by-

(I) any authorized institution;

(II) any bank incorporated outside Hong Kong which is not an authorized institution;

(III) any controller or director of the company;

(IV) any relative, within the meaning of section 79, of any such controller or director;

(V) any firm, partnership or body corporate in which the company, any controller or director of the company or any relative, within the meaning of section 79, of any such controller or director, is interested as director, partner, manager or agent;

                 (VI)   any holding company, subsidiary or associated company of the company;

                 (VII)   any subsidiary or associated company of any such holding company; and

        (B)   total assets (less contra items) of not less than $4,000,000,000 or an equivalent amount in any other approved currency; and

    (iii)   it has been a deposit-taking company or a restricted licence bank (or any combination thereof) for not less than 10 continuous years.

EIGHTH SCHEDULE

[ss. 22(1) & 135(1)]

GROUNDS FOR REVOCATION OF AUTHORIZATION

1. In this Schedule, "controller" includes a minority shareholder controller.

2. The Monetary Authority is satisfied that, if the authorized institution were not authorized and were to make an application under section 15 for authorization in respect of the business referred to in that section presently being carried on by it, section 16(2) would prohibit him from so authorizing it (but excluding the criteria specified in paragraphs 2(b) and 13 of the Seventh Schedule).

3. The Monetary Authority is satisfied that the authorized institution proposes to make, or has made, any composition or arrangement with its creditors or is insolvent or is being or has been wound up or is otherwise dissolved.

4. The authorized institution has made a report to the Monetary Authority under section 67 that it is likely to become unable to meet its obligations or is about to suspend payment or the Monetary Authority is satisfied that the institution is so unable or has suspended payment.

5. The Monetary Authority is satisfied that the authorized institution has not provided him, whether before or after being authorized, with such information of a material nature relating to it, and to any circumstances likely to affect its method of business, as is required under this Ordinance.

6. The Monetary Authority is satisfied that the authorized institution has provided him, whether before or after being authorized, with information which is, to a material extent, false, misleading or inaccurate, and whether or not such information was so provided pursuant to a requirement under this Ordinance.

7. The Monetary Authority is satisfied that the authorized institution has contravened any condition attached under section 16 of this Ordinance to its authorization.

8. The Monetary Authority is satisfied that the authorized institution has-

> *(a)* in the case of a bank, ceased to carry on banking business;

> *(b)* in any other case, ceased to carry on a business of taking deposits.

9. The objects of the authorized institution as stated in its memorandum and articles of association or other document constituting the company no longer include the object of-

> *(a)* in the case of a bank, carrying on banking business;

     (b)   in any other case, carrying on a business of taking deposits.

10. The authorized institution has failed to pay any fee required by section 19 to be paid by it after being advised in writing by the Monetary Authority that it is contravening that section.

11. The authorized institution has failed to comply with any requirement under section 60 applicable to it after being advised in writing by the Monetary Authority that it is contravening that section.

12. In the case of an authorized institution which is a deposit-taking company or restricted licence bank, the institution has contravened section 14(1) or (3).

13. A person has become a controller of the authorized institution after having been served with a notice of objection, within the meaning of section 70, objecting to his becoming such a controller.

14. A person continues to be a controller of the authorized institution after having been served with a notice of objection, within the meaning of section 70 or 70A, objecting to his being such a controller.

15. A person has become or continues to be a chief executive or director of the authorized institution in contravention of section 71.

16. The authorized institution is in contravention of section 74.

17. The authorized institution engages in business practices specified in a notice under section 82(1).

18. The Monetary Authority is satisfied that the interests of depositors or potential depositors of the authorized institution are in any other manner threatened by the institution continuing to be authorized.

19. The authorized institution requests in writing the Monetary Authority to revoke its authorization and the Monetary Authority is satisfied that the interests of depositors of the institution are or will be adequately safeguarded if he complies with that request.

20. The Monetary Authority is satisfied that the authorized institution engages in business practices which would be likely to prejudice the interests of Hong Kong as an international financial centre.

NINTH SCHEDULE

[ss. 53C(I)(b) & 135(3)]

POWERS OF MANAGER OF AUTHORIZED INSTITUTION

1. Power to take possession of, collect and get in the property of the institution and, for that purpose, to take such proceedings as may seem to him expedient.

2. Power to purchase property for the institution.

3. Power to sell or otherwise dispose of the business or property of the institution by public auction or private contract.

4. Power to raise or borrow money and grant security therefor over the business or property of the institution.

5. Power to appoint a solicitor or accountant or other professionally qualified person to act for the institution.

6. Power to exercise any voting rights in respect of any shares which-

      (a)   in the case of an institution incorporated in Hong Kong, are owned by the institution;

      (b)   in the case of an institution incorporated outside Hong Kong, are an asset of the institution's principal place of business in Hong Kong or of any local branch.

7. Power to bring or defend any action or other legal proceedings in the name and on behalf of the institution.

8. Power to give guarantees in the name and on behalf of the institution.

9. Power to refer to arbitration any question affecting the institution.

10. Power to effect and maintain insurances in respect of the business or property of the institution.

11. Power to use the institution's seal.

12. Power to do all acts and to execute in the name and on behalf of the institution any deed, receipt or other document, including power to enter into, carry out, assign or accept the assignment of, vary or rescind, any contract, agreement or other obligation.

13. Power to draw, accept, make and endorse any bill of exchange or promissory note in the name and on behalf of the institution.

14. Power to appoint any agent to do any business which he is unable to do himself or which can more conveniently be done by an agent and power to employ, direct and dismiss employees.

15. Power to do all such things (including the carrying out of works) as may be necessary for the realisation of the property of the institution.

16. Power to make any payment which is necessary or incidental to the performance of his duties and the exercise of his powers.

17. Power to carry on the business of the institution.

18. Power to grant or accept a surrender of a lease or tenancy of any of the property of the institution, and to take a lease or tenancy of any property required or convenient for the business of the institution.

19. Power to make any arrangement or compromise on behalf of the institution.

20. Power to call up any uncalled capital of the institution.

21. Power to rank and claim in the bankruptcy, insolvency, sequestration or liquidation of any person indebted to the institution and to receive dividends, and to accede to trust deeds for the creditors of any such person.

22. Power to change the situation of the institution's business office.

23. Power to do all other things incidental to the exercise of the powers specified in this Schedule.

TENTH SCHEDULE

[ss. 60(1) & (11) & 135(3)]

NOTICE RELATING TO AUTHORIZED INSTITUTION'S

AUDITED ANNUAL ACCOUNTS

PART I - Publication Of Notice

The notice shall be published in one English language newspaper (and in the English language unless otherwise approved by the Monetary Authority) and one Chinese language newspaper (and in the Chinese language unless otherwise approved by the Monetary Authority), each of which shall be a newspaper circulating in Hong Kong.

PART 2 - Matters To Be Contained In Notice

The notice shall contain-

(a)   a copy of the institution's audited annual accounts for the financial year to which the notice relates;

(b)   a copy of the report of the auditors pursuant to section 141 of the Companies Ordinance (Cap. 32);

(c)   the full and correct names of all persons who are directors or managers for the time being of the institution; and

(d)   the names of all subsidiaries, for the time being, of the institution.

Hong Kong as a Tax Haven for International Business

by

Adam Starchild

Tax havens are very much in the news, and stories about small- and medium-sized companies mushrooming overnight and multi-national giants amassing fabulous fortunes via tax haven operations are growing. They may sound like Alice in Wonderland fairy tales to most people, but to the sophisticated entrepreneur, use of foreign tax havens for such advantages is an everyday business opportunity.

The use of a foreign corporation domiciled in any one of the famous company tax havens such as Hong Kong, Panama, the Bahamas, or Bermuda (among others, can enhance the profitability of any international business.

Many European and American companies are expanding and diversifying overseas as a means of growth and as a hedge against economic ups and downs in their country of origin. By incorporating a tax haven operation to accumulate tax-free income, accomplishment of multi-national objectives is accelerated. An international trading or freight operation can be established in a tax haven to be used as a conduit for international sales activity and financing. Such operations can accumulate trade discounts, commissions, advertising allowances, etc., completely tax-free while the parent or associated company can assume tax deductions by absorbing administrative and selling costs.

Before getting into the ways in which tax haven operations are used by various types of businesses, it is of eminent importance that the distinct difference is understood between two seemingly similar terms: "tax avoidance" and "tax evasion." Tax evasion has dubious and illegal overtones: for example, a company might falsify its financial statements so as to conceal its full liability to the tax authorities — that would be tax evasion — an infraction of the law and a very serious one.

Tax avoidance, on the other hand, is a legitimate method of minimizing or negating the tax factor. In simple terms, it is utilizing "loopholes" in tax laws and exploiting them within legal perimeters. This is the cornerstone of the tax haven concept.

Certain offshore companies can defer any tax until the profits are repatriated to the investor's home country. These are generally companies actively engaged in the conduct of a local business. In most import-export or other international trade activities, such a definition is especially easy to meet. A retailer, or group of retailers, could set up their own wholesale buying opertion in a convenient tax haven, such as Hong Kong, and put all of their Asian business through it. The profits of the Hong Kong firm would accumulate tax-free, and could be invested in other foreign operations.

223

In addition, a great many countries offer tax holidays of 5 to 20 years for new export manufacturers or assembly operations, often including smaller companies down to as few as ten employees. A company or group of companies could easily invest some of their foreign profits in such a venture, continuing to build for tax-free profits. Such concessions often include an exemption from customs duties on raw materials and equipment.

Most developed countries do tax the current income of certain types of corporations controlled by their residents, such as leasing companies, and other financial enterprises dealing the parent company. But this concept of a controlled foreign corporation applies usually to passive or tax-haven type corporations, not to active businesses. But even for a passive business, a joint venture with foreign partners on a 50-50 basis will allow the income to accumulate tax-free since the company is not controlled by national of either country. If you are leasing equipment, consider a joint venture with your foreign partner whereby you set up a jointly owned company to receive some of the income. You will both profit by it, and have a tax-free pool of funds to invest together in other ventures. Such profits will not be taxed in the country of either partner until they are repatriated, since they are not controlled by either country's citizen.

Countries which have no income tax include Bermuda, the Bahamas, the Cayman Islands, Nevis, and the Turks & Caicos Islands. A number of countries do not tax foreign source income, including Panama and Hong Kong.

Many businessmen looking for tax haven opportunities would envy the daily opportunities open to international traders, and yet most international traders rarely use these opportunities — or even understand them. 100% tax-free dollars will grow a whole lot faster than 50% after-tax dollars.

Setting Up Your Tax Haven-Based Trading Operation

A firm I can personally give my highest recommendation to is ICS Trust (Asia) Limited, based in Hong Kong.

The handover of the former British Crown Colony of Hong Kong to China is complete, and it is now called the Hong Kong Special Administrative Region, generally abbreviated to Hong Kong S.A.R., even on official documents.

As more than one local businessman has put it, "now that the politicians and journalists are gone (from covering the handover), we can get down to *business*." This attitude is typical of Hong Kong, still a true capitalist center. In fact, many of the wealthy who left to obtain second citizenships in Canada, Australia, and elsewhere, have now returned home to continue building their fortunes.

The major advantage of Hong Kong is simply that it is a real business center, not just a tax haven. One of the consequences of that is the ability to add value to services that are provided in only skeleton form in other tax havens. The reinvoicing business is a prime example. Most tax haven jurisdictions host a number of trading companies that do nothing more than reinvoicing. But one Hong Kong firm has now developed this traditional service into a "real" business mode, with an ability to arrange local trade financing. This is a healthy step away from traditional tax havenry into a true offshore **business** center.

ICS Trust Company Limited is part of the ICS International group of companies headquartered in Hong Kong. This highly successful entrepreneurial group was started by Elizabeth L. Thomson. Elizabeth describes herself as "a lawyer by profession" (2 law degrees, a member of 4 Law Societies internationally), "an entrepreneur by choice"! She has helped innumerable people start new enterprises in many parts of the globe and is well known in Hong Kong for her work with women entrepreneurs.

With a staff of 40 at ICS, every aspect of your business is covered — from deciding to incorporate, to obtaining financing from the bank, to managing your paper work including Letters of Credit, to investing your hard earned profits! ICS is truly a "one stop shop" for entrepreneurs.

Their clients range from multinational companies for whom they run Direct Import Programs worth millions of dollars to individuals who seek tax sheltering and estate planning on an international scale. As an entrepreneurial group, they attract many entrepreneurs as clients — business people who have grown their business to a level of maturity and profits that requires expansion into Asia for many diverse reasons.

Instead of just a paper thin traditional tax haven reinvoicing company, with ICS you can develop a real business in Hong Kong. With their extensive banking contacts, ICS professionals will "shop" for the best letter of credit facilities that Hong Kong's competitive banking scene can offer, likely better facilities than you can find at home. Depending upon the client, ICS can often arrange letter of credit banking facilities for clients with either a low or zero margin deposit, usually required by the opening bank. By freeing up your collateral and capital, they provide you with more purchasing power to increase sales and gain higher profits.

Most of these reinvoicing transactions are usually effected such that they are tax free in Hong Kong. There is no withholding tax on dividends so it is often possible to engage in international trade through a HK company and obtain dividends from that company tax free.

ICS will also work with international banks and factors in Hong Kong and overseas to arrange financing, secured primarily on the strength of purchase orders from your clients. Working with banks, factories, shipping companies and freight forwarders, ICS will structure a transaction to increase the likelihood of obtaining flexible, low cost facilities.

The goods do not need to go through HK for us to use a HK vehicle to pass title. Most of their clients ship from a third country direct to their own country.

Although the traditional Hong Kong focus is on firms who trade in goods, it is also possible to use these structures in cases where services are to be provided from overseas. For example, a firm could contract out a study to a company in Hong Kong. This Hong Kong company could then sub-contract out the work to a third party firm and the profit kept in Hong Kong, tax free.

If you import goods from Asia for sale to large chains, ICS can help you expand your credit facilities and increase your domestic sales by establishing and running a Direct Import Program for you. Combined with their international trade finance capabilities, the Direct Import Program is a powerful tool for generating more profits.

The primary goal of the Direct Import Program is to maximize your profits by making your customers perceive that they are buying "direct." This is achieved by:

- setting up a subsidiary company in Hong Kong
- getting your buyers to open their L/C or orders to this subsidiary
- liaising with suppliers to ensure goods are to specification.

The Direct Import Program works because of two powerful reasons:

- The trend in the retail industry is for buyers to "buy direct" from the Orient. Having a subsidiary in Hong Kong which receives orders or L/Cs greatly enhances this perception.

- Large retail chains often can obtain freight and insurance at significant savings because of their economies of scale. Selling FOB Asia can often result in a lower selling price for the importer but with the same profit.

ICS will set up and manage the subsidiary company for you, and prepare financing proposals for presentation to local banks. When everything is complete, goods are shipped directly from the Asian factory to the customer. The fact that you are now seen as an Asian supplier (and not the middleman) is often an important factor that clinches the deal. The added prestige of a Hong Kong office makes the customer think he or she is buying "direct" and therefore receiving the lowest price.

To get started, you should contact ICS with as much detail as possible about your business and its trading activities.

For further information, contact:

> Mr. Kishore K. Sakhrani, Director
> ICS Trust (Asia) Limited
> 8th Floor, Henley Building
> Five Queen's Road, Central
> Hong Kong
> Telephone: +852 2854 4544
> Fax: +852 2543 5555

You will be well-advised and well-serviced in the hands of this fine company.

Sources of Help for Offshore Investing

Britannia Corporate Management Limited

Another business specializing in the formation of offshore corporations and trusts is Britannia Corporate Management Limited, located in the Cayman Islands. Its president, Gary F. Oakley, is a Canadian with over 18 years of Cayman Islands residency. Britannia is licensed to manage investment holding and trading companies, real estate holding companies, patent holding companies, and insurance holding companies. It is licensed to incorporate and manage corporations registered in the Cayman Islands. As such, the firm can service as the registered office of a corporation, provide its secretary, officers and directors, or undertake any day-to-day functions that may be required. More information can be obtained by writing the following:

> Britannia Corporate Management Limited
> Attn: New Clients Information
> P. O. Box 1968
> Whitewall Estates, Grand Cayman
> Cayman Islands

Britannia can be reached by fax at +1 345 949 0716, marking your fax "Attention New Clients Information.

Skye Fiduciary Services Limited

Skye Fiduciary Services Limited are among the foremost experts in offshore planning. Under the direction of its chairman Charles Cain, formerly managing director of the second merchant bank to open in the Isle of Man, Skye Fiduciary is the most experienced offshore corporate and trust management business in the jurisdiction. Although Skye offers a full range of company and trust management services, their expertise in designing novel company structures to meet the needs of foreign clients is unique.

For further information, write the following:

Skye Fiduciary Services Limited
Attn: New Clients Department
2 Water Street
Ramsey, Isle of Man 1M8 1JP
United Kingdom

Their telephone number is +44 1624 816117. Fax service is available at +44 1624 816645; marking your fax "Attention: New Clients Information".

JML Swiss Investment Counsellors

One of the leaders in Swiss financial management is JML Swiss Investment Counsellors, a firm which offers a unique style of financial management. Clients can customize and control their own portfolios and still receive comprehensive management advice from some of the world's best experts on financial matters.

Recognizing that investors have differing goals, time frames, and tolerance for risk, JML's managers work with their individual clients to help them target their unique objectives. This naturally requires continued surveillance and analysis of worldwide economic trends, political events, financial markets, currencies, and other factors which could make some investments particularly attractive and others most unfavorable. Few individuals have the time or expertise to undertake this kind of evaluation themselves.

Further information about JML can be obtained by writing the following:

JML Jurg M. Lattmann AG
Swiss Investment Counsellors
Germaniastrasse 55, Dept. 212
CH-8033 Zurich, Switzerland

Their telephone number is (41) 1 368-8233 and their fax number is (41) 1 368-8299, marking your fax "Attention Department 212".

Weber Hartmann Vrijhof & Partners

While there are many excellent Swiss investment financial managers, another one of particular note is the management firm of Weber Hartmann Vrijhof & Partners. Offering management services for the portfolios of both individuals and companies, the firm excels at providing personal attention to its clients. Weber Hartmann Vrijhof & Partners was established in 1992 by Hans Weber, Robert Vrijhof, and Adrian Hartmann. The three men have substantial experience in finance and investment. Weber managed Foreign

Commerce Bank (FOCOBANK) in Switzerland for nearly 30 years as its president and CEO, Vrijhof was a former vice-president and head of FOCOBANK'S portfolio management group, and Hartmann was head of FOCOBANK'S North American subsidiary in Vancouver. Weber Hartmann Vrijhof & Partners offers specialized investment services designed to meet the individual needs of their clients.

The minimum opening portfolio to be managed by this firm is $250,000 or equivalent. The management team here normally recommends that a portion of the portfolio be invested in hard currencies other than the U.S. dollar including the Swiss franc, French franc, German mark, and Dutch guilder. Respected for their conservative approach to portfolio management, the partners assist clients with opening a custodial account at one of the major private Swiss banks, so that all client securities are held by the bank, not the investment manager.

A large percentage of their clients are based in the United States. One of their main goals has always been to get a certain portion of their clients' wealth out of the U.S. dollar and into European hard currencies such as Swiss francs, Deutschmarks, and Dutch guilders, and then build a portfolio with a mix of bonds and shares.

For more information, you can write to the following:

Weber Hartmann Vrijhof & Partners Ltd.
Attn: New Clients Department
Zurichshstrasse 110B
CH-8134 Adilswil, Switzerland

Their telephone number is (41-1) 709-11-15 and their fax number (41-1) 709-11-13, marking your fax "Attention New Clients Department".

Dunn & Hargitt International Group

Recently, many international investors have become dissatisfied with the small annual return on Euro-dollar deposits.

This is why private and institutional investors throughout the world are looking at other areas where returns can be in the area of 20-25% a year, to help offset the high annual rates of inflation on luxury goods.

The Dunn & Hargitt International Group, founded in 1961, has specialized in doing research for developing Portfolio Management Programs that have the potential of providing investors with a high return on their capital by investing in a diversified portfolio trading in the commodity, currency, precious metals, and financial futures markets in the United States and throughout the world.

The Dunn & Hargitt group offers investors the possibilitiy of participating in several of the different pools that are managed by them by investing through the investment programs that are offered by their affiliate, Winchester Life in Gibraltar, but which are actually managed by The Dunn & Hargitt International Group.

At the time of publication they are offering three possible investment alternatives, including The Winchester Life Umbrella Account (which allows 100% of a client's money to be invested in a diversified futures portfolio), The Winchester Life 100% Guaranteed Investment Account (in which Lloyds Bank acts as custodian trustee and US Government Zero Coupon Treasury Bonds are set aside to guarantee the client's capital), and The Winchester Life 150% Guaranteed Investment Account (which is a similar program, but guaranteeing that the client will receive at least 150% of the value deposited with a maturity date at least ten years in the future).

The average net return for the 150% Guaranteed Investment Account over the last six years would have been 22% a year. The average net return on the 100% Guaranteed Investment Account over the last six years would have been 27% a year. The average annual net return for The Winchester Life Umbrella Account over the last twelve years would have been 35% a year.

The minimum accounts accepted are $20,000 for The Winchester Life Umbrella Account, $20,000 for The Winchester Life 100% Guaranteed Account, and $50,000 for The Winchester Life 150% Guaranteed Account.

Although commodities are a speculative form of investment, investors everywhere are diversifying part of their portfolios to take part in the considerable potential profit opportunities that are available in the commodity, currency, precious metals and financial futures markets. The programs devised by the Dunn & Hargitt International Group will make profits if significant trends develop in either direction; i.e. up or down. This does not mean that short term results are always profitable, however the Dunn & Hargitt proven trading systems can provide above average returns over the longer term. Their objective is to make a profit for their clients of between 20% and 40% per annum and their computer trading systems are geared to this level of performance.

For more information, contact:

The Dunn & Hargitt International Group
c/o Dunn & Hargitt Research S.A.
Department S-697
P.O. Box 3186
Road Town, Tortola
British Virgin Islands

The structure of the Dunn & Hargitt Group has been established so that no taxes are withheld from the client's investment on the international commodity, currency, precious metals and financial futures markets. Because of this they can only manage money for investors who are neither citizens nor residents of the United States.

The Dunn & Hargitt International Group offers complete confidentiality to all of its clients, and will not reveal any information on a client or on its accounts to any third parties.

About the Author

This special afterword was prepared by Adam Starchild who over the past 25 years has been the author of over two dozen books, and hundreds of magazine articles, primarily on business and finance. His articles have appeared in a wide range of publications around the world — including *Business Credit, Euromoney, Finance, The Financial Planner, International Living, Offshore Financial Review, Reason, Tax Planning International, The Bull & Bear, Trust & Estates*, and many more.

Now semi-retired, he was the president of an international consulting group specializing in banking, finance and the development of new businesses, and director of a trust company.

Although this formidable testimony to expertise in his field, plus his current preoccupation with other books-in-progress, would not seem to leave time for a well-rounded existence, Starchild has won two Presidential Sports Awards and written several cookbooks, and is currently involved in a number of personal charitable projects.

His personal website is at http://www.adamstarchild.com

www.ingramcontent.com/pod-product-compliance
Lightning Source LLC
Chambersburg PA
CBHW051210200326
41519CB00025B/7065